ENDORSEMENTS FOR
I Don't Love You

This book is going to send shudders do
therapeutic community. It will make
make them mad. But in the process it will force everyone to recon-
sider how he or she advises couples processing the pain of adultery.
For any woman who's been through the pain of betrayal, or any
man who's put her through it, this book is a "must read" primer for
restoring love, intimacy, and trust.

> — Dr. Tim Kimmel
> Exec. Dir. of Family Matters
> Author of *Basic Training for a
> Few Good Men*

Finally, a no-wimp, hard-hitting, beyond-tough-love, biblical
approach in dealing with the devastation of an affair. David Clarke's
method may appear to be too harsh, but it's based on the truth of
God's Word. That's why it simply works! Every married couple and
single adult contemplating marriage should read this book to help
affair-proof their marriage. It is an absolute must for Married
couples who have faced an affair.

> — Jay Dennis
> Pastor of Church at the Mall,
> Lakeland, Florida
> Author of *The Prayer
> Experiment* and *Taming Your
> Private Thoughts*

In a culture that throws away relationships like paper cups, David Clarke clearly shows not only how to fight for your marriage—but how to do so biblically. Clarke makes it clear that when a spouse says those dreaded words, "I don't love you anymore," the most loving response is to lovingly but firmly rub your mate's nose in the truth—the truth of covenant in marriage and the consequences of breaking covenant. Clarke does a masterful job of outlining, chapter by chapter, the game plan for dealing with a spouse who has lost that lovin' feeling.

— Rod Cooper, Ph.D.
Kenneth and Jeanne Hansen
Professor of Discipleship and
Leadership, Gordon-Conwell
Theological Seminary

It was a pleasure to read Dr. David Clarke's book *I Don't Love You Anymore*. It is a book that doesn't mince any words or worry about who might be offended at hearing the truth. In my nearly thirty-two years of practicing law, I have seen all too many books that dance around the issue and just say that if everybody can just love everybody, everything will be all right. It isn't that way and it isn't that simple, and Dr. Clarke tells it like it is.

— John A. Grant
Executive Vice President,
Government and Legal for
Liquidmetal Technologies

"Direct, blunt, extremely tough, revolutionary, and biblical!" That describes David Clarke's latest work that could potentially reduce the workload of divorce attorneys! If you think your partner doesn't love you anymore, don't give up until you read this book!

— Claudia and David Arp
Marriage Alive Seminars
Authors of *10 Great Dates* and
The Second Half of Marriage

WHAT TO DO WHEN HE SAYS,

I DON'T

LOVE

YOU ANYMORE

*An Action Plan to Regain Confidence,
Power, and Control*

DAVID CLARKE, PH.D.

THOMAS NELSON
Since 1798

NASHVILLE   DALLAS   MEXICO CITY   RIO DE JANEIRO   BEIJING

Published in Nashville, Tennessee, by Thomas Nelson, Inc.

Library of Congress Cataloging-in-Publication Data

Control Number: 2002111398
ISBN-10: 0-7852-6515-5
ISBN-13: 978-0-7852-6515-3

Printed in the United States of America

07 08 09 10 RRD 10 9 8 7 6

I dedicate this book to Bill Clarke:

marriage and family therapist,
my dad, my mentor, my editor,
and a man who loves
the Lord Jesus Christ.

Dad, you've taught me so much
about counseling couples in crisis:

that sin must be confronted and the truth
must be told if change is to occur.

Thanks for all your work on this book. We did it together.
I know it is your prayer, as it is mine,
that this book will provide hope,
practical help, and healing to those
whose partners don't love them anymore.

CONTENTS

CONTENTS

PART 1

WAKE UP!
YOUR SPOUSE
WANTS OUT

ONE

A Classic Case of Hit-and-Run

What "I Don't Love You" Really Means

You're walking alone in your neighborhood on a beautiful, sunny afternoon. The sun is warm, the flowers are blooming, and the breeze feels good. You feel confident, secure, and safe. Suddenly, you hear behind you the sound of an engine revving and wheels squealing. You turn and see with horror a car hurtling down the quiet street right at you. It must be going seventy miles an hour! You're in the middle of the road, and there's nothing you can do. There just isn't time. Just before impact, you notice it's one of your cars and your husband is behind the wheel!

The car slams into you with a sickening crunch and you flip into the air, smashing into the windshield and then crashing to the pavement in a heap. With your face pressed to the gritty tarmac, you watch the car scream around the corner and disappear from sight.

You're stunned, dazed, bleeding, and confused. As you lie there, all twisted and broken, questions flood your mind: *What happened? Was that really my husband? Why would he run me over? Why won't he stop and come back? There must be some mistake! What do I do now?*

No, there's no mistake. That was your husband, and he meant to run you over. He's not going to stop. He's not going to say he's sorry. In fact, he thinks he had every right to run you over.

I know that was a pretty graphic story, but this scene is a pretty good description of what it's like to hear from your husband's lips: "I don't love you anymore." Maybe he hasn't said these exact words to you, but his behavior screams out that he doesn't love you. He has run you over, and you don't even know why. The reasons he gives you make sense to him, but not to you. You've got to get up, get off that road, and get moving. You need to bind your wounds, protect yourself, and pull your life together.

The first step in healing is to push past your shock and denial and face the truth. If you can clearly understand three brutal, ugly realities, you can get up and begin your journey back to sanity and strength. And you'd better get up and out of that road, or he'll come back and run you over again . . . and again . . . and again.

I want to be perfectly clear on something right up front. Throughout this book, I refer to the husband as the one who is the adulterer or involved in some other significant sin. The only reason for this is to avoid the awkward switching back and forth between the masculine and feminine pronouns: *he/she, him/her.* Obviously, the wife could be the one who says, "I don't love you anymore," and is sinning.

TURN OUT THE LIGHTS; THE PARTY'S OVER

First of all, you must understand exactly what "I don't love you anymore" means. It does not mean any of these things:

- "I'm unhappy, but I still want our marriage to work."
- "I want to get my love for you back."

- "If we get some help, maybe we can save the relationship."

- "I'm confused and not sure what I want."

- "If you make some changes, I think we'll be okay."

There are no *if's*, *maybe's*, or *we'll see's* about it. It is not a cry for help. It is a cry of finality. It is a slamming door.

Here's what "I don't love you anymore" really and truly means:

- "I've had it with you and our marriage."

- "Our marriage is over."

- "I've thought this through very carefully and I'm not changing my mind."

- "I have a plan of escape mapped out and I'm going to follow it."

- "I am divorcing you."

He's not kidding. He's not trying to get your attention. He has decided to get out of the marriage. Period. In a high percentage of cases, he also has found someone else he'd rather be with.

As I explain the tough-as-nails approach they must take in response to an unloving husband, many of my female clients say, "But if I'm too tough, I'll scare him off!" My response is always the same: "You can't scare him off because he's already gone." These clients desperately want to believe he's teetering on the fence. He's not. He jumped off the fence and is five neighborhoods away.

Oh, he may act confused and all torn up inside. Don't buy it. A lot of these husbands ought to receive Oscars for their "this really hurts me" performances. The pain you see is either fake, or just the last few gasps of guilt for what he's going to do. The guilt won't stop him. All he's worried about now is how to get away from you with the least amount of damage to his reputation and bank account.

WHERE'S THE COMMITMENT?

The second unpleasant reality is the state of marriage. American society used to value highly the institution of marriage. People revered it as one of the pillars upon which this country was based. When you got married, you were expected, by practically everybody, to stay married. There was a tremendous amount of healthy social pressure—from government, church, business, media, school, neighborhood, friends, and family—to work through the tough times and remain husband and wife. Unless you had an extremely good reason, divorce was not an option.

Oh, how the times have changed. In the 1960s society's commitment to marriage began to erode. In the 1970s and 1980s, this erosion became a landslide. We now stand at a point in American history where there is no commitment at all in secular culture to lifelong marriage. Zero. Zilch. The value of marriage has been buried under an avalanche of secular excuses, rationalizations, New Age psychobabble, and selfish lusts.

Marriage has become another casualty of the world system. More accurately, Satan's system. We did not heed God's warning in 1 John 2:15–17:

Do not love the world, nor the things in the world. If anyone loves the world, the love of the Father is not in him. For all that is in the world, the lust of the flesh and the lust of the eyes and the boastful pride of life, is not from the Father, but is from the world. And the world is passing away, and also its lusts; but the one who does the will of God abides forever.

Marriage has gone from being a permanent and essential home fixture to a temporary convenience. It's like an appliance—the refrigerator, the stove, or the dishwasher. As long as it works and meets your needs, fine. When it begins to break down and give you trouble, just get rid of it and get a new one.

Divorce used to be the last and worst alternative to continuing in a troubled marriage. Now it is considered the first and best alternative. Every single divorce has the world system seal of approval on it. The message trumpets from every corner of society: "If you're in pain, in conflict, or just not in love anymore, then get out of the marriage and get out quickly while you're still young enough to attract another partner. You're only going to live eighty years, so you might as well be happy. You're a fool if you stay!"

There's still plenty of support for marriages in the church. Wherever God's Word, the Bible, is faithfully taught, there will be Christians who will help you in your time of crisis. They'll genuinely want you and your spouse to stay together. They may not give you the best advice in the world. They may not have the guts to confront your husband, but at least you will benefit from their love and encouragement.

Unfortunately, the church will have little influence on your husband. By definition, he has rejected God and isn't interested in church or spiritual things. Oh, he may continue to play church, but the truth is, he has chosen to be sucked into the world and its beliefs. And the world says to him, "Welcome home! It's great to have you back. You're doing the right thing by getting rid of your marriage. Look at all the fun activities available to you." It's music to his old nature ears.

I'm not telling you this to discourage you. I just want you to realize that you can't depend on society, or even your church, to change your husband. It's going to be up to you. With God's help, and backed by a very small band of loyal supporters, do what you can.

I'M MARRIED TO AN ALIEN

The third truth you must come to grips with is the most painful one: *this is not the man you married.* Your loving, kind, and loyal spouse is gone. In his place is this stranger. You've never met this person. If you didn't know better, you'd say an alien has taken over the mind and body of your husband. And this alien is not nice.

Your new husband is cold, mean, devious, manipulative, and 100 percent selfish. He has no sympathy or compassion. He couldn't care less what you think and feel. His determination to meet his selfish needs is destroying your marriage, your family, and your dreams. You can't believe how he looks at you or how he treats you. Is this man the same person you married? No, he is not. And the sooner you realize this, the better off you and your marriage will be.

A huge part of your denial is thinking you're still dealing with your same old husband. Here are some of the favorite excuses (and my responses) from women who think they're living with the man they married:

CLIENT: I think he really wants to save the marriage.

ME: No, he doesn't. He wants to end it.

CLIENT: He's so stressed at work lately . . . maybe that's it.

ME: We're all stressed at work. Stress doesn't cause what you're seeing. I'm stressed at work, too, but I'm not walking out on my wife. He's walking out on you because he wants to.

CLIENT: He's confused.

ME: No, he's not. He knows exactly what he wants.

CLIENT: He's still living with me, though. Surely, that's a good sign.

ME: That means nothing. It's cheaper and more convenient than a hotel or apartment. He's only using your home as his temporary headquarters. He has planned his escape, believe me.

CLIENT: This is just not like him! This is my fault! I must have made some mistakes to cause him to act this way.

ME: Stop beating yourself up. This is all about him, not you. It's his fault for turning his back on you and God. I'm sure you haven't been a perfect wife, but that's no excuse for the sinful choices he's making.

As a clinical psychologist who's seen hundreds of couples in therapy, I've had a lot of experience with husbands (and wives) who have become aliens. I've talked to them. I've looked into their eyes. I've heard their rationalizations, distortions, and lies. They're in their own little worlds, their own private realities. Satan has fooled them into believing that what they're doing is right. The trouble is, they don't know it. They are completely deceived, and no one can convince them that the path they're on will destroy them. They just don't get it.

• • •

The spouse who wants out has a very clear, very carefully planned agenda. He wants to retain the upper hand and stay in control of your relationship. By keeping you confused and emotionally distraught, he feels better about himself and what he is doing. Your ragged ups and downs and feeble efforts to win him back confirm that divorce is the only option. I mean, why would anyone want to stay with a pathetic basket case like you?

He will assure you of his deep regret for the pain he is putting you through: "Honey, I'm sorry this is happening. I feel terrible seeing you so miserable." Baloney! Most of the time he wants you to be in pain. The more depressed and weak you are, the better divorce deal he is going to get. You're thinking only of saving the marriage, and he is adding up dollars and cents! I've known plenty of persons who meticulously plotted to overwhelm their spouses so they could win custody of the kids.

Even if he actually does feel your pain, that's no comfort. He is still causing you terrible pain, and he has no intention of stopping.

The real skill is in smashing the spouse to bits without seeming to do so. Some are brazen and crude about it, but most are clever and subtle. One of the classic techniques is the "let's be friends" approach to divorce. He sadly admits that he doesn't love you and the marriage has to end, but that's no reason why you can't be friends. He wants you to agree that you both tried, but your marriage just didn't make it. If you play along and act like a real chum, he comes out smelling like a rose! You have legitimized your own divorce.

Grasping these three harsh realities will help propel you past your denial, bewilderment, and pain. By the time your partner runs you over, you are way behind in the race to salvage your marriage and family. You've got to catch up and make an impact on your overconfident, determined, and possibly soon-to-be ex-spouse. You can do it with a series of decisive steps. What kind of steps? Read on.

TWO

DESPERATE TIMES DEMAND DESPERATE MEASURES

Getting Past the Shock and Getting Your Spouse Back

I closed the door of my therapy office, and my new client took a seat on the couch. She immediately burst into tears, sobbing quietly as she rocked back and forth. Several minutes and four tissues later, she finally composed herself and told me her story:

> I can't believe it! I just can't believe it! I never dreamed I'd be sitting with a Christian psychologist talking about my marriage. My friends, people at church, and my family will be amazed to find out Bill and I are having problems. Everybody thinks we have the model marriage. *I* thought we had the model marriage. Last Wednesday night, after the kids were in bed, Bill turned the television off and said he had something to tell me. I knew when he turned the television off, it was serious. He looked me right in the eyes and said, "I don't love you anymore."

She began crying again, harder this time. There are no words more painful to hear from your spouse than "I don't love you anymore." As she cried, I thought about all the clients

I've worked with who suddenly found themselves in the same situation. Without warning you discover you are no longer lovable. You are being unceremoniously dumped by the person who promised to love you and live with you forever. It's not forever yet, is it?

"I DON'T LOVE YOU ANYMORE" IS AN EPIDEMIC

My client is not experiencing a unique, exceptional circumstance. The "I don't love you anymore" nightmare is an epidemic sweeping across America and the world. Thousands—tens of thousands, hundreds of thousands—of married persons' lives and relationships are being ripped apart with these five simple words. And sad to say, the numbers for Christian and non-Christian couples aren't very different. Being married to a Christian and attending church do not guarantee your partner's love will make it to the marital finish line.

The partner who no longer loves you will break the bad news in a variety of ways. The basic message, however, is the same: "It's over, and I want out." Here are the most popular statements used to end a marriage:

- "I don't love you anymore."
- "We've grown apart."
- "I never loved you."
- "I felt pressured to marry you."
- "We are two different persons."
- "Persons just can't change."
- "I feel trapped."
- "I need space."

- "I need to find myself."
- "It's not you; it's me."
- "I'm just not good for you."
- "I'm so bored with my life and our relationship."
- "You're not intellectually challenging."
- "I've grown beyond you."
- "I'm having a midlife crisis."
- "I love you like a brother [or a sister]."
- "I love you as the parent of our children."
- "I love you, but I'm not in love with you."
- "I don't love you the way a spouse should love you."
- "I think God wants me to be happy."
- "It's better for the kids because our bad marriage is hurting them."

All these marriage-ending statements are cop-outs, rationalizations, and outright lies. Not to mention insulting, unbiblical, dishonoring to God, and just plain stupid. The problem is, the person laying these ridiculous comments on you actually believes them, which makes them even more devastating to the hearer. The hearer's response usually sounds something like this:

I had no idea this was coming. No idea at all. It's like he walked up and dropped an atom bomb in my lap. I thought things were fine. Not great maybe, but okay. Life has been hectic lately with the kids and our jobs and the finances. We haven't been as close, I admit that. But still . . . it hasn't been that bad! How could he do this to me? To us?

BEING WEAK AND PASSIVE IS THE NATURAL RESPONSE

When your spouse tells you that the love is gone, you are traumatized in every sense of the word. There is no more brutal form of rejection. Your life is in pieces, and you have no clue what to do. What to say. How to attract your partner back and save your marriage. You are shocked. Stunned. Horrified. In absolute disbelief. Your mind can't seem to grasp what's happening. You're in denial. You're in grief. You're in a fog. You're in a panic. You're overwhelmed.

To put it bluntly, you are a mess—a mixed-up, confused, shell-shocked, quivering, emotionally strungout mess. That's why you will, most likely, do everything wrong in your frenzied efforts to win back your partner's love and commitment.

You'll cry. You'll act weak, desperate, and guilty. You'll beg, whimper, and plead. You'll blame yourself for the fact that your partner doesn't love you anymore. In an attempt to gain control in an out-of-control situation, you'll magnify your weaknesses and promise to change overnight. You'll think, *If I'm the problem, everything will be okay when I change.*

You'll promise to do anything—anything at all—to please your partner and motivate him to stay in the relationship. You'll go into hyperdrive as you try to overwhelm your partner with love and attention. You'll talk with your partner about your relationship all the time. You'll ask him again and again why he doesn't love you. You'll say, "I love you," twenty times a day and wait expectantly for him to respond, "I love you too."

You'll touch him often and offer to have sex every night. You'll even tell him you're willing to do whatever he wants you to do sexually. You'll go on a crash diet and begin a rigorous exercise regimen. You'll tell him you're not sure you can go on if you lose him.

And you'll be wrong. Wrong. Wrong. Wrong. All wrong! Not only will you humiliate yourself, but you'll lose any chance to save and rebuild your marriage. You'll end up divorced. You'll think you're doing the best you can do to win your partner back. The truth is, you'll be doing the worst you can do. You'll be doing what comes naturally, but it will kill your marriage. You'll drive the last few nails into the coffin of your relationship.

Incredibly, this weak, passive approach I've just described is the most popular and most recommended marriage-saving advice in the Christian community. The vast majority of Christian therapists, pastors, and authors actually believe that you should chase a partner who no longer loves you. They think you ought to do everything in your power to love your partner back.

There's just one problem with this advice. It doesn't work. These "experts" ought to know better. This self-flagellating, boot-licking, walk-on-me-because-I'm-a-doormat approach is nothing less than a disaster. It never works. It never has, and it never will. The only thing it's good for is ending your marriage.

"I Don't Love You Anymore" Is a Sin Problem

The reason it doesn't work is that it's not biblical advice. It's not what God wants you to do when your partner wants out of your marriage. My strategy in this book is based on my firm belief that a spouse who says, "I don't love you anymore," is in serious sin.

He is violating God's commands concerning the sacred covenant of marriage. His behavior will devastate you, deeply wound your children, and destroy your family. It's very likely he's in an affair or engaged in some other sinful behavior. If he is a Christian, he's clearly out of fellowship with God. He has turned his back on God, and he is in Satan's camp.

When a man is sinning in this catastrophic way, his sinful

behavior is the only issue. This is *not* a marriage problem. It is a sin problem. In these desperate circumstances, you don't try to improve the marriage. You try to get the man to stop sinning.

All the usual "please try to save your marriage" verses do not apply to your situation. Submit to your husband (Eph. 5:22–24; 1 Peter 3:1–6) does not apply. Respect your husband (Eph. 5:33) does not apply. Turn the other cheek (Matt. 5:39) does not apply.

The verses that do apply to the "I don't love you anymore" nightmare, as they do to all serious sin, are Matthew 18:15–17:

> If your brother sins against you, go and show him his fault, just between the two of you. If he listens to you, you have won your brother over. But if he will not listen, take one or two others along, so that "every matter may be established by the testimony of two or three witnesses." If he refuses to listen to them, tell it to the church; and if he refuses to listen even to the church, treat him as you would a pagan or a tax collector. (NIV)

God does not want you to work on your marriage now. God does not want you to passively allow your husband to annihilate himself and all you hold dear in the world. God wants you to confront your sinning husband the *Matthew 18* way. This book will show you exactly how to do that. You'll find a complete explanation of the biblical support for my approach in Chapter 12.

How to Bring Your Marriage Back from the Dead

It's just about impossible to find a book that provides realistic, practical, and effective help when you're told you are not loved anymore. Most marriage books promote the passive, pitiful approach to marital reconciliation, or they simply aren't written to address a crisis situation. Your basic marriage book, even if it's good, is written for couples who still have an intact relationship. You know, a five or six on a scale of ten. When your marriage is at zero, the "let's see if you can improve your relationship" approach isn't helpful. It's like tossing a children's aspirin tablet to a woman with a gaping chest wound. You don't have a marriage. It's over. The only question is: Can you bring it back from the dead and start over? If your marriage is at zero, this book is for you.

> Dr. Clarke, I want to save my marriage. I still love him. I want him back. I don't want to be divorced. I don't want to be a single mom. I don't want the kids to suffer, and I know they will. Is there a chance for us? What can I do?

I'll tell you what I told this client. It's the same thing I've told thousands of clients and thousands of people in my seminar audiences over the past fifteen years:

Yes, there is a chance. Your husband may not be in an affair. But your marriage is over. That much is certain. There is a way to breathe new life into it, however. I can't offer you any guarantees, but my approach will give you the best opportunity to get your husband back and start a brand-new marriage. My way is not the easy way. It's the tough way. But I believe it's God's way for your situation. I'm going to ask you to do things that will feel unnatural, harsh, even cruel. Desperate times demand desperate measures.

I'm going to take you step-by-step through a process that will give you strength, power, and confidence. It will balance the marital scales and earn back the respect of your husband. It will help you draw close to God. It will save you, it will save the kids, and it might just save your marriage. My approach is rough. Aggressive. No holds barred. It's beyond tough love. I call it

Matthew 18 love. You're on the defensive now, reeling from the blows your husband has landed. That's over. It's time to fight back. Fight back hard and smart.

The rest of my book contains the details of my Matthew 18 love plan. I cover the two classic "I don't love you" scenarios:

"I DON'T LOVE YOU, AND I'M HAVING AN AFFAIR"

Ninety percent of "I don't love you" spouses are having an affair or are on the verge of beginning one. You need to find out if your spouse is on the verge of beginning one. You need to find out if your spouse is in an affair (if you don't already know). You need to motivate him to stop it and to want you back. You need to heal from the affair's damage and take your marriage from the ashes to complete recovery. You can still have God's best for your marriage after an affair, and I'll show you how to do it.

"I DON'T LOVE YOU, AND I'M NOT HAVING AN AFFAIR"

How many women are married to husbands who do not love them? Who do not talk personally? Who are about as romantic as a block of wood? Who are selfish? Who meet only their own needs year after year after year? Who are addicted? Who are abusive? Too many to count. If you're in this kind of a loveless, unsatisfying marriage, it's time for a change. You need to stop tolerating his lack of love. You need to stop enabling him to be a poor husband. You need to take decisive action to make him uncomfortable and maybe motivate him to make some changes.

Please keep in mind that I'm going to talk to you as I talk to my clients. I'm going to be direct, blunt, and aggressive. I'm going to cut to the heart of the matter and tell you exactly what to do in response to a spouse who doesn't love you. I do not intend to be insensitive or offensive, although at times you may think me to be both. My goal is to get your attention and motivate you to take the correct actions.

THREE

"HELP! IS MY SPOUSE HAVING AN AFFAIR?"

*Look for Evidence
and Go on the Attack*

There's no sense in beating around the bush. When you hear "I don't love you anymore" from your spouse, it usually means he's having an affair. Not always, but usually. If he's not in love with you, chances are, he's in love with someone else. Or he thinks he is. Ninety percent of the time a third person is involved, and some kind of a romantic relationship has developed.

I know you don't want to believe this. After reading that first paragraph, you thought, *No! No, that's not true! I'm sure he's not having an affair. I'd know if that was happening.* No, you wouldn't know. The spouse is usually the last to know because you don't want to see it. And the folks who know haven't told you because they are "sparing your feelings." But burying your head in the sand won't do you or your marriage any good. Take my advice and assume he's having an affair.

Keep in mind, it doesn't have to be a full-blown sexual relationship to qualify as an affair. Here's my definition of an affair: any emotional involvement between a married person and a member of the opposite sex that is *clearly* beyond a reasonable business and/or social level. If your husband has any kind of an inappropriate, deeper-than-a-friend-or-coworker emotional connection with another woman, then he's in an affair.

Affairs always start off innocently enough. No one's planning to have sex. Oh, they'll end up in bed, all right. But not right away. The game has to be played first. They get that initial tingly feeling during a conversation in the break room, at the gym, at a party, or at church. Longer, more in-depth conversations follow. They begin sharing how unhappy they are in their jobs, lives, and marriages. They're still just good friends at this point. Yeah, right.

Then they plan to meet and talk. Lunches together follow. Phone calls multiply. And then there's that first physical touch, and both "friends" feel the electricity. They share their real feelings for each other and talk about how they really shouldn't be getting this close. They're in too deep now, and both know what's going to happen. More passionate and intimate touch happens, followed pretty quickly by intercourse.

Now, you tell me. At what point is this relationship an affair? Okay, I'll tell you. It's an affair from the very beginning. From the moment your husband chooses to pursue a deeper relationship with another woman to whom he is attracted, he has started an affair. The last time I checked, sin is sin, and it doesn't matter to God where you are on the slippery slope. You shouldn't be anywhere near the slope! Satan is a master at the subtle art of orchestrating an affair. He knows just when a husband or a wife no longer loves a spouse, and he moves quickly to bring along an attractive, sympathetic, and willing person of the opposite sex. Presto! It's an affair.

SHERLOCK HOLMES IS ALIVE!

It's extremely important to find out whether your spouse is in an affair. Every day the affair continues, there is less chance your marriage will make it. If he is involved with someone else, exposing that sinful relationship is a critical opening step in the recovery process. Suddenly, his affair becomes the issue, and the spotlight is no longer on your perceived inadequacies as a spouse. The light of truth is shining on him and his sin. Now there's a chance for genuine brokenness, repentance, and the renewal of your marriage. It will begin with his leaving his paramour and working hard to win *you* back.

The very first thing you need to do when you think there's an affair is to hit your knees and ask for God's help. Pray that God will reveal the affair to you. The second thing is to ask your close friends to pray that if there is an affair, it will come to light. The third thing you need to do is to gather up your courage and, with Jesus Christ by your side, confront your spouse. Ask him directly and firmly if he is having an affair. Use my broad definition to cover any loopholes. Sometimes a partner who would never admit an affair will acknowledge an inappropriate relationship. He'll say something like this: "Well, I do have a friend. She's only a friend, and we've had some good talks." Bingo! She's the paramour.

To get any kind of an admission, your approach must be confident, strong, and assertive. If you ask in a shaky, halting voice with big tears in your eyes, he'll never tell you. He'll think that you're too weak to take the truth and that it'll push you over the edge. Convince him you're tough enough to take it. Act angry, cold, and forceful. Press him for an honest answer. Use words like these:

Bob, I have something very important to ask you. I want a straight answer, and it better be the truth. Do not lie to me. Do you have any emotional attachment to a member of the opposite sex that is beyond a reasonable business or social level? You've made it clear you don't love me anymore. So, who are you involved with?

It's a good idea to ask specific questions:

- "Are you talking on a personal level with any member of the opposite sex?"
- "Is anyone becoming more than a friend?"
- "Are you calling anyone just to chat?"
- "Have you gone out to lunch with anyone?"
- "Have you touched another woman in an intimate way?"

Bring up changes in his behavior and lifestyle you've noticed. Tick them off one by one and see what kind of reaction he gives you:

- "You're working out more."
- "You've lost weight."
- "You're really watching your diet."
- "You've bought new clothes in different styles."
- "You've changed your hairstyle."
- "You've picked up a new hobby."
- "You've bought a new car."
- "You're not wearing your wedding ring."
- "You're listening to music you never listened to before."
- "You've got a whole new set of friends."
- "You're spending more and more time with your new friends."
- "A lot of your time away from home is not accounted for."

These are classic symptoms of a person having an affair. If he doesn't love you anymore, it's pretty obvious he's not making these changes for you. Tell him you know something's going on and you want answers.

Sometimes, acting as if you know he's had an affair will force an admission. Walk up to him, and in the coldest voice you can muster, say, "I've been doing some investigating. I know what you're doing. You have one day to tell me the entire truth. One day to save your marriage." Then turn and walk away. Unless he breaks and confesses his sin, do not communicate with him or do anything for him over the next twenty-four hours.

Don't be afraid to confront the affair issue. Many of my clients fear that they'll make a bad situation worse by asking about an affair. That's simply not possible. The situation is already as bad as it can be. If he's not in an affair, you've lost nothing. He doesn't love you anyway. Confronting him about an affair builds respect points for you. It may help him realize how vulnerable he is. It's also part of your campaign to fight back. And don't forget: there's a 90 percent chance you're right and he is in an affair.

If you have any fear that your husband will react violently to your confrontation, don't do it alone. Ask at least two friends, one of whom should be a man, to join you. They can attend the meeting or be in the next room.

If, as is very likely, he denies an affair, go into a detective mode. Don't obsess over the situation and become consumed by it, but do take a number of prudent investigative steps:

- Go through his wallet, briefcase, and desk.
- Go through any drawers where he keeps personal papers.
- Go through his car with a fine-tooth comb.
- Go over every inch of your bedroom.
- Go through the garage and any other storage areas.

- Check all phone records, including cell, home, and his office numbers, for the last few months.

- Check the money trail: ATM withdrawals, checking and savings accounts, credit card bills.

- Check your home computer for his e-mail history and the Web sites he has visited.

- Ask your good friends (very good friends) to tell you if they know anything and to keep their eyes and ears open.

- Ask a good friend to follow him for a few days. If these steps yield no evidence, consider hiring a reputable private investigator.

Many supposed experts counsel against looking for evidence of an affair. They actually think you're better off not knowing. The truth is, if you don't try to find out, you'll always wonder. You won't gain any respect in his eyes. You have no chance to get his attention and shake him out of his "I don't love you" mode. Plus, if he's in an affair and you don't find out, your marriage and family will be destroyed.

If there's a strong suspicion that someone has committed a murder, the police look for evidence. Well, your spouse may have murdered your marriage, and you need to look for evidence.

If your spouse catches you playing detective, offer no apologies. Hold your head up and say, "What am I supposed to think? The way you're acting, I believe you're having an affair, and I'm going to find out. Until you genuinely love me again and our marriage is healed, I'll always wonder."

If you're absolutely confident there is no affair, skip to Chapter 5 now.

If You Want Me Back, You Better Get to Work

When the affair is out in the open, you need to swing into high gear. You will be devastated at the news, of course, but you cannot afford to stay devastated. You've got to dry your tears, hitch up your pants (or your pantyhose), and go on the attack. Get mad and stay mad. Anger is a God-given emotion that provides you with the strength and motivation to act in a crisis.

You won't feel like acting with anger and decisiveness, but you simply must if you hope to save your marriage. If you have to fake it, fake it. I guarantee you that if you fail to face your spouse's affair in an aggressive way, disaster will result. You won't heal from the trauma. Your husband won't heal from what he has done to you, to your family, to himself, and to God. And last but not least, your marriage will be over for good.

It's possible that if you remain weak and wimpy in the aftermath of your spouse's affair, he'll come back to you. But you'll stay married in name only. It will not be a pleasant existence. There will be no resolution. No trust. No respect. No new marriage. In fact, chances are very good he'll have another affair. He got away with it!

You'll never know why he had the affair. You'll never know exactly what happened in the affair. You'll never know if you're loving him enough to keep him from another woman. You'll never know if he truly is sorry for what he did and has recommitted his heart to you.

You'll never know if he really loves you. The pressure is all on you. You can live this way if you want to. I don't recommend it, and I don't think God recommends it. God says sin is to be confronted so the sinner can repent and be restored (Matt. 18:15–17).

Some of the worst marriages I see in therapy are those with

unresolved affairs. The affair might have been over for twenty years, but it makes no difference. It's as though it just happened last week. The pain, agony, and betrayal are still fresh. The marriage is being eaten away from the inside.

My approach works! It can help you heal from an affair and build the brand-new marriage God wants you to have. I believe so strongly in my affair recovery program that if a couple refuse to follow it, I won't continue to see them.

When you discover the affair, you do not forgive quickly or easily. You'll eventually forgive, but not right away! You are angry. You are outraged. You are deeply wounded. You are downright mean. You make your spouse's affair the number one and only issue. Down the road, you'll be more than happy to deal with your personal issues and the marital issues. But not until you've seen considerable effort and progress from your adulterous spouse.

There will be no "I love you's." No "I forgive you's." No "I know we're going to make it's." It's far too soon for that. What there will be is you fighting back and turning the tables on your unfaithful spouse. Until the affair is exposed, it's "Oh, no, I'm losing Bob!" With the affair out in the open, it's "Bob, you've lost me unless you work like a dog to win me back."

Go to the phone and call a small group of close friends. Call your pastor too. Tell them about the affair. Ask them to start praying, harder than they have ever prayed, for you and your spouse. Then get down to business.

The first thing you need to know is how *not* to deal with an adulterous spouse. There are some classic mistakes you cannot afford to make. Once I've covered what not to do, I'll teach you what I believe God wants you to do when faced with the trauma of adultery.

PART 2

"I DON'T LOVE YOU, AND I'M HAVING AN AFFAIR"

FOUR

WIMPS
FINISH LAST

How Not to Deal with
an Adulterous Spouse

My 10:00 A.M. appointment with a married couple I was seeing for the first time began as the two settled on my couch. The woman's face looked strained and desperate, as though she were holding up a huge wall of terrible pain. She'd been crying and looked to be on the verge of bursting into tears again. The man was calm, composed, and relaxed. He seemed cold, indifferent, and strangely detached from both his wife and me. He crossed his legs and glanced at his watch, as if to say, "Come on. Let's get this over with."

I started the session by getting a little history. Both were in their middle thirties. Married almost fifteen years. Two children. Good jobs. Both professed to know Jesus Christ personally and were regular, active members in a local evangelical church. Their lives seemed to have been happy and good until recently.

I asked, "What brings you in to see me today?"

The wife turned to her husband and began to cry quietly. He looked me right in the eyes and, in a flat voice devoid of any emotion, said, "I've had an affair." No guilt. No shame. No quavering voice or hanging head. All very bad signs. His message was as clear as though he'd actually said the words: "I'm not ashamed, and I don't want to give up this new woman."

The rest of the story was as disgusting as it was predictable. He'd met her at work, and at first, they'd just been friends. She was attractive, cheerful, and just fun to be around. Slowly, step-by-step, they got closer—emotionally and then physically. They'd been involved sexually for about the past two months. The wife had found out last Tuesday when she'd discovered a hotel receipt in his briefcase. The affair was still going on. He said he hadn't slept with this woman for a week but was still talking to her at work and on the telephone.

EXCUSES, EXCUSES, EXCUSES

He launched into the usual idiotic excuses and rationalizations: "I'm in love with this woman. I never really loved my wife and shouldn't have married her. We're just so different. I believe God wants me . . ."

I cut him off at that point and said, "That's enough. Save the excuses. What you're doing is wrong. It's sin. You need to stop the affair immediately and follow the steps I'm about to give you. If you follow my program, God will forgive and bless you. God will help you build a brand-new marriage from the marriage you've wrecked. If you choose to continue the affair, God will not overlook your sin, and there will be serious consequences. Your marriage will be destroyed. Your family will be destroyed. And you will be destroyed. Which way do you choose to go?"

He was shocked and became angry. He said he couldn't believe I would treat him in such a blunt, harsh way. He expected empathy, sympathy, or some kind of understanding. I told him I was talking to him the way God would talk to him: in an honest, truthful, and loving way. I said my affair program was the best thing *for him*. He didn't believe me. In a huff he got up and stalked out of my office.

His wife moaned, "I can't believe he left."

I replied, "He left you a few months ago. Here's what I want you to do if you want to protect yourself, protect the children, and have the best chance to bring your marriage back from the dead." Step-by-step, I went over my entire Matthew 18 program. The first step I recommended was to kick him out of the house if he didn't make a complete turn around in twenty-four hours.

"Be a Wimp and Hope for the Best"

After hearing me out, she looked down and whispered, "I just can't do it. It just seems too tough, too much of a risk. I've talked to my pastor, and he urged me to take an entirely different approach." Even though I had a pretty good idea what this approach was, I asked her to tell me his suggestions.

It was, as I had suspected, the classic "be a wimp and hope for the best" strategy. She told me her pastor wanted her to forgive her husband for the affair and not bring it up again. He thought that her husband might have had the affair because he wasn't happy at home. So, he instructed her to be the best wife she could be and pursue him: be cheerful, be affectionate, make nice meals, be romantic, invite him often to have sex, ask what his needs are every day, and really work hard on her weaknesses. Her pastor thought by doing all these behaviors she'd be able to steer her husband back towards herself and away from the other woman.

Hearing this, I had a strong urge to throw up. Instead I said to this dear lady as gently and firmly as I could: "Your pastor is a good man. A nice man. A godly man. A well-meaning man. And he is an absolutely, 100 percent wrong man. He's not malicious; he's just clueless. Out of a genuine concern to save your

I DON'T LOVE YOU ANYMORE

marriage, he is giving you unbiblical advice. It's not your job to win your husband back. It's his job to win you back." I ended the session by telling her I respected her decision to follow her pastor's guidance. I told her to call me if she wanted to see me again.

THE TERRIBLE PRICE WIMPS PAY

Two months later, the same woman called and returned to my office. She told me, through tears, a story I've heard too many times to count. She said she wished she'd followed my approach because her pastor's advice had proved to be disastrous. The more she tried to please and pursue her husband, the more he pulled away from her. He got meaner, more arrogant, bolder in his sin, and drew even closer to his paramour. The marriage was definitely over. Her husband had decided to move out of the house a month ago, and she'd received the divorce papers last week. But the end of the marriage wasn't the worst of it. Not by a long shot.

By playing the passive, eager-to-please wimp, my client had done a great deal of damage to herself. She was nothing less than emotionally devastated. She was clinically depressed and struggling just to maintain a basic level of functioning. She found it increasingly hard to keep up with the children and their activities, go to the store, prepare food, pay bills, and perform other chores she used to do easily. Her grief was overwhelming her. She had allowed herself to continue to be her husband's victim. Her self-esteem had been decimated. Her confidence was gone. She was not ready, physically or emotionally, to rebuild her life.

It dawned on her, too late, that by trying so hard to change herself and convince her adulterous husband to love her again, she had actually confirmed to him that *she* was the reason the marriage had failed. She had made herself the issue rather than his horrific sin. The central issue—in fact the only issue—should have been his adultery! As she deteriorated emotionally, her wonderful husband convinced many of their Christian friends and fellow church members that she had been a rotten wife and was unstable. Since she refused to tell others about his affair, he had ample opportunity to lie and deceive and win them to his side. When she did finally reveal his affair, many of her former friends didn't believe her.

Perhaps the worst blow of all was the damage she unwittingly did to her relationship with her children. They saw her tolerate their dad's daily mistreatment of their mother and his wife. They saw her desperate attempts to motivate him to care about her. They saw her sadness and tears and inability to care for them in a competent, assertive way. And so they did what most children do in these circumstances: they lost respect for her and began to mistreat her. They lost faith in her as a secure, stable parent. They became depressed and began to act out at school and at home.

To her horror, her kids got closer to her husband and expressed a desire to live with him after the divorce. Emboldened by her passivity and their increasing allegiance to him, her husband was now fighting for primary custody.

Finally, her behavior in response to his affair ended up leading her husband deeper and deeper into sin. In a sincere attempt to save her marriage and do what was right, she unwittingly helped him along the way to destruction. By failing to confront and expose his sin, she emboldened him to continue in it. Her husband seemed happy and content, but in reality he was rotting away on the inside. His fellowship with his heavenly Father had ceased. Eventually, in a year or two, he would probably realize how foolish he'd been to trade his precious wife and spiritually intact family for cheap, temporary, sexual thrills. But by then it would be too late. He'd have to suffer the painful consequences of his actions for the rest of his life.

Believe me when I tell you that this woman is not the exception. Hers is not an isolated, special case. What happened to her is what happens to 80 percent of my female clients who choose the weak, passive response to a husband who commits adultery. I could tell you hundreds of stories just like hers. If you're going to play the pathetic, "Please love me again," "What have I done wrong?" "How can I change?" wife to your adulterous husband, you're going to get it in the neck just as this woman did.

In the other 20 percent of cases where the wife makes the same mistakes as this client did, the husband ends up dropping his paramour and the marriage survives. But all the damage I described still happens. The marriage is still over. It's a lifeless, passionless, miserable marriage. No respect. No trust. No forgiveness. No intimacy. No real change. Just two damaged persons barely surviving in an atmosphere poisoned by doubt and hurt and betrayal.

GOD WANTS YOU TO CONFRONT YOUR PARTNER'S SIN

Now, you tell me. Is this kind of human emotional and spiritual carnage what God wants? Is it His desire to see all this pain and misery? Do these results glorify Him? No, of course not! Does God approve the weak, passive response to adultery that directly causes these results? No, He doesn't! God does not support an intervention strategy that is the equivalent of tossing a drowning person a one-hundred-pound block.

Many Christian authors, psychologists, leaders, and pastors honestly believe being a wimp is the correct biblical answer to an adulterous spouse. No, it's not biblical. In fact it is the *opposite* of what God teaches in His Word.

Nothing is clearer in the Bible than the nature of sin. It is seen in the incredible cost provided for its forgiveness—the death of God's Son. It brought eternal death and separation from God to all men. It is repugnant to God. To ignore or enable sin is precisely what God never does and what Scripture does not describe. God does not want us to ignore or enable sin. He wants us to confront sin in a direct, assertive way (2 Sam. 12:7; Matt. 5:23–24; 18:15–17; 2 Cor. 13:2; Gal. 2:11; 2 Thess. 3:14–15; Titus 3:10–11).

My beyond tough love approach is biblical and, therefore, the approach to follow. I sincerely believe it is God's approach. And it all begins with anger. Your God-given, righteous anger at your adulterous spouse will give you the strength and determination to follow my affair recovery program. Your anger will be the battering ram that punches through your husband's wall of sin and denial and forces him to his knees before God. If you want real change in your husband and your marriage, you'd better get angry.

FIVE

"BE ANGRY, AND YET DO NOT SIN"

Anger Is Your Friend in a Marital Crisis

(Note to the reader whose husband is not having an affair: I want you to read this chapter and Chapter 6, even though my focus is how to get angry at an adulterous spouse. Your situation is just as serious. Though your husband has not committed overt sexual sin, he doesn't love you and he is sinning. And you need to get angry.)

There are thirty minutes left in my first session with a wife who just found out about her husband's adultery. She has described what she knows so far about the affair, and I've covered the specific steps in my affair recovery program. As I finish the last point of my program, I notice a certain familiar look on her face. I know what she's going to say. It will be a dialogue I've had with hundreds of wives in my office. Here's how it goes:

WIFE: Oh. Oh, my! You want my husband and I to do all those things? I mean, all of them?

ME: Yes, I do.

WIFE: Well, I . . . I don't think I can be strong enough to follow through.

ME: What do you mean, not "strong enough"? [Actually, I know what she means.]

WIFE: I'd have to be really angry to carry out your program.

ME: You're exactly right. To do what I'm asking, you'll have to be good and angry. In fact you'll have to be angrier than you have ever been in your life.

WIFE: But I'm not that angry.

ME: You're not that angry? I'd hate to see what he'd have to do to get you angry. He has slept with another woman, lied about it, refuses to tell you details about the affair, thinks saying, "I'm sorry," is enough, wants you to just get over it, and isn't sure he wants to come to therapy. Doesn't all that make you angry?

WIFE: I was angry at first, but . . . not anymore. Now I'm more sad and hurt.

ME: Sad and hurt is not going to help you, him, or the kids. Sad and hurt will get you divorced or stuck in a loveless, trustless marriage. Grieving is important, but you can grieve later. Anger is what you desperately need, and you need it now.

WIFE: But, Dr. Clarke, you don't understand. I still love him, and I don't want to lose him. How can I get angry at a man I've loved and given my life to for so many years?

ME: Here's what I understand. He doesn't love you anymore, and you've already lost him. As we sit here, he's a goner. He has no respect or love for you. To get him back, you need to be angry. If you don't get angry, your marriage is over—whether he divorces you or not. Plus, you'll be emotionally disabled and have a terrible time rebuilding your life.

WIFE: I don't know if I can get angry at him.

ME: My job is to help you get angry and stay angry so you can follow my program, which I believe is the only way that offers hope for the marriage.

You ought to feel the kind of anger that Jesus felt when He saw His house (the temple) made into a den of robbers, when it should have been a house of prayer. Your marriage, a sacred institution established by God, has been desecrated by your husband. If ever there was a time for righteous anger, this is it!

I know some of my advice will sound unchristian to you. Trust me, that's only because you've been misinformed about how Christians are supposed to behave when dealing with sin.

WHY WIVES HAVE TROUBLE GETTING ANGRY

So many affair victims are just like this wife. They do get angry, but it peters out very quickly. After a brief burst of fury, they turn all weepy and wimpy. They're too nice. Too forgiving. Too sweet. Too sympathetic. Too passive. Too depressed and devastated. If they keep running down this "anything but anger" path, it's going to be too late to save their marriages.

There's only one way you can motivate your husband to work with you to create a new, healthy marriage out of the ashes of the one he destroyed. You must produce sustained, intense anger. That's easy for me to say, but very difficult for you to do. Like my client, you need to know three things about anger: (1) why you're having trouble getting and staying angry, (2) why anger is so important in the affair recovery process, and (3) how to get angry and stay angry at your adulterous husband. I'll explain these first two in the remainder of this chapter, and then tackle the third in the next chapter.

"I'm in Shock"

When you first discover his adultery, you immediately move into the stage of shock and denial. You simply cannot believe it's true. Not your husband! He wouldn't do this to you! You might waste several weeks stumbling around in a confused, dazed fog. It's easy to get stuck in this stage because you're trying to protect yourself. You don't want to believe what's happened. Deep down, you may feel that you're not ready to face the truth and the terrible pain that comes with it.

Even when you accept the reality of his affair, it's common to think and act in ways that shield you from the emotional pain. You'll tell yourself that everything is really okay. What happened is not that bad, and you're sure things will be just fine in no time. You'll believe his lies about how involved he was with this woman because you want to. You are still trying to come to grips with what your mate has done to you, and you're not there yet.

You'll try to convince yourself you're not angry. Affair victims tell me all the time: "I'm not angry, just sad and disappointed." Baloney. You're angry, all right. You just don't want to feel your anger because it will force you to come face-to-face with harsh reality. If you're really angry, then that means he's done something really wrong.

In an instinctive—and quite normal—attempt to minimize the damage and not take his behavior personally, you'll make ridiculous excuses for your husband's affair: "Well, Fred had a bad childhood," or "Fred's going through a midlife crisis."

My response is: "Who cares? There's no excuse for what he's done." You need to take his affair personally because it *is* a personal attack on you. He prefers another woman to you! I say that's personal.

Here's an example that shows you just how strong the denial

urge is. I was winding up my first session with a wife and her husband. During the session, I had found out all kinds of nasty things about the husband. He was a chronic liar and manipulator. He was incredibly selfish and would turn on his smarmy charm only to get something he wanted from her. He had engaged in multiple affairs. He had forced his family into financial ruin. He was emotionally abusive to her just about every day: hateful, belittling, critical. This poor, codependent wife actually asked me, "How can I know for sure he doesn't love me?" I said, "You're kidding, right? Will it take his sticking a knife into your guts and twisting it to make you realize he hates you and wants to destroy you?"

Your denial is perfectly normal. It is a God-given, natural defense mechanism that automatically kicks in if you discover your spouse has committed adultery. Everyone goes through denial. My job is to push you as hard as I can to get out of denial as quickly as you can. Strength, confidence, and recovery begin when you get out of denial and into anger.

"I'm a Nurturer"

The very nature of a woman will get in the way of getting angry. You are sensitive. You are forgiving and sympathetic. You are a servant, a supporter, and a helper. As his wife you are used to being unselfish and making sacrifices for him. You give more than he does. You pursue him more than he pursues you. And so, when you are faced with the crisis of his infidelity, you automatically go into your natural nurturing mode. You do what you've always done: you reach out in a caring, giving way with no consideration of your own feelings and needs. It's an expression of your love, and it's also an attempt to get him to love you back. It might work with your basic, regular husband. It is not only useless but disastrous when used with an adulterous husband who doesn't love you anymore.

As the nurturer you're thinking, *I can change him if I just love him enough.* No, you're wrong. The usual ways of loving will cost you respect and push him farther away. You might be able to engineer change with a tough, merciless, aggressive love. This is not the time to be sweet and nice. Don't put on your fake pearls and high heels and knock yourself out meeting his needs. It's time to be Joan of Arc. Strap on your armor, adjust your metal-plated pantyhose, take your sword in hand, and go into battle.

"I Feel Guilty"

One of the adulterous husband's most diabolically clever rationalizations is to blame his affair on his wife. He'll say, with a straight face and a tone dripping with just the right amount of fake sadness and sincerity, "If you'd been a better wife, if you'd met my needs, I wouldn't have had the affair." Instead of laughing in his face, his wife takes this monstrous lie to heart and believes it! By playing the guilt queen, you play right into his sinful hands. If he can get you to take any part of the blame for his affair, he's sitting pretty. He believes he's in the clear. He's gotten your seal of justification. He doesn't have to be sorry. He doesn't have to stop the affair. He doesn't have to change. He doesn't even have to feel bad about divorcing you.

Wives buy into this guilt complex for several reasons. First, poor self-esteem. Women tend to be too hard on themselves. Women are much more in touch with their faults than men are with theirs. When he points out weaknesses you know you have, he has a good chance of tapping into your guilt. Affair victims will often admit to me: "I *am* overweight." "I didn't keep a very tidy house." "I didn't show as much interest in sex as I could have." "I *did* spend too much."

Second, the wife is desperate to draw her husband back to her and their relationship. She'll do anything to get him to work on the marriage, so she's often eager to admit her faults. She'll say to him, "I'm at fault too! Let's work together on my problems and your problems."

Third, an admission of partial blame for his affair is an effort by the wife to exert some kind of control over the situation. If she persuades herself that she helped cause his affair, then she believes she has the power to win him back. She thinks, *If I'm at fault, then all I have to do is change and he'll love me again,* or *If I improve in my areas of weakness, that's what he wants. He'll stop the affair and want to be with me.*

Accepting guilt for his affair is simply not true to the facts. You have exactly zero responsibility for his affair. It's 100 percent his fault! He has to answer to God for any behavior he chooses. Here's how I respond to a wife who is willing to bear and acknowledge *any* guilt whatever:

WIFE: I feel guilty for his affair. I think I did play a part in it.

ME: Did you have the affair?

WIFE: No.

ME: Did you set him up with this sleazy woman?

WIFE: No, of course not.

ME: Would it be your fault if he went out and burglarized a home or killed someone?

WIFE: No.

ME: Well, all right then. The affair is all his fault. Any behavior he adopts is his total responsibility. If you'd been the worst wife in the world, it would still be his fault. If you accept any blame, you'll be under tremendous pressure even if he stays in the marriage. You'll have to wonder every day of your life if you're doing enough to keep him happy and away from other women.

Accepting guilt for your husband's affair also lets him confuse the real issue. The real issue—the only issue—is his affair! *First*, the affair work must be done. The affair must end, respect must be reestablished, the paramour must be flushed out of his heart, and healing must take place. *Later*, if he earns the right, the two of you can focus on the marriage and changes both need to make.

You're 50 percent responsible for any marital issues, but that's a completely separate category from his affair. If he has the gall to so much as whisper one of your weaknesses before he has helped you heal from his adultery and betrayal, feel free to blast him with some righteous anger. Tell him to shut up, sit down, say he's sorry and mean it, and be glad he still has a chance to stay married to you.

"I'm Scared"

The sheer intensity of the rage you feel will frighten you. You've never been even close to feeling so much anger before. You're scared of what you might do if you express it. You convince yourself that this kind of anger is overkill. It's far beyond normal. It's not ladylike. It's not Christlike. You must be the one at fault. But that's what you think. Based on this line of reasoning, you stuff your anger down deep inside. You suppress it. You ignore it. It's still there, but you pretend it's not.

Your anger isn't the only thing you fear. You have a terrible and realistic fear of losing everything and everyone you hold dear. Your husband. Your marriage. Your dignity. Your way of life. Your financial security. Contemplating all these losses is overwhelming. Your husband has put all of these valuables at risk, and your reaction is to be paralyzed with fear. Instead of fighting back, it's very easy to pretend you're not angry and to do nothing.

"The Christian Community Tells Me, 'Don't Be Angry'"

Commitment to marriage in the evangelical culture has never been lower. Oh, the right things about marriage are said in our churches. God's teaching about the sanctity of marriage is heard quite often in sermons and seen in Sunday school lessons and bulletin inserts. But hardly anyone has the intestinal fortitude, the spinal column strength, to back up these pious pronouncements with biblical *action.*

I've had hundreds, thousands, of clients tell me they received no help from Christian brothers and sisters in dealing with an adulterous spouse. They went to Christian family members, friends, pastors, counselors, elders, deacons, and fellow church members. They asked if someone—anyone—would confront the spouse and try to turn him from his sin. You know, do what it says to do in the Bible. They got very few takers. It's amazing how many Christians become gutless wonders in the middle of a marital crisis.

In Matthew 18:15–17, the steps of confrontation are laid out clearly. First, you confront your husband alone. If he refuses to listen, the second step requires you to take one or two persons and confront him again. If he still refuses to stop sinning, then it's the responsibility of the church leaders to inform the entire church of his sin. If he continues to sin, everyone in the church must cut him off and ignore him.

In our current church culture, it is usually not the adulterous spouse who is ignored. Scripture is ignored. These verses in Matthew 18 are among the most disobeyed in the Bible. Perhaps when biblical church discipline became virtually a thing of the past, these verses went with it—or the disobeying of the verses precipitated the virtual end of church discipline. It is very difficult and painful to confront someone involved in adultery, but that's what God commands all of us to do.

The party line you're given is to be a patsy. Don't get angry because that's sinning and will make matters worse. Try to be gracious, caring, understanding, and submissive. Forgive him, and do all you can to work on the marriage. Just hang in there and hope for the best.

These dear Christian souls don't want to get involved. They don't want to offend the sinning partner. They don't want to be uncomfortable. They will say that God has forgiven your husband. Why can't you?

These concerned members of the body of Christ will pray for you. Thanks a lot. You're drowning, and they're standing on the bank watching you and praying. As you slip beneath the waves, you'll be comforted with the thought that your Christian support team is praying for a miracle. Prayer is important, but it is not enough.

Why Anger Is So Important

Even after my brilliant explanation of the obstacles to anger, my client wasn't completely convinced that she had to get angry at her husband.

"Are you sure?" she asked.

I replied, "Yes, I'm sure. I know anger is an absolute necessity in your circumstances." Here are the reasons I gave her.

First, anger is a normal, healthy, God-given reaction to a traumatic event. The initial shock and denial suppress your anger. The anger is there, and you need to get to it because it's how you begin to respond assertively to a serious threat.

Your husband's adultery certainly qualifies as a threat to every area of your life. His choice to do this to you is a horrible betrayal by someone who pledged his lifelong love to you alone. God gives you anger to help mobilize your physical, emotional, and spiritual resources to deal with the horrific, life-shaking trauma of his adultery. While it is true that, with your anger, there is profound hurt and pain, these emotions won't help your husband or the marriage's chances. Obviously, he was willing to subject you to such excruciating emotional pain.

Second, getting angry at your adulterous husband is good for you. Without the full and proper expression of anger, you'll never forgive him, not because you don't want to, but because you won't be able to. God designed anger to come first in response to trauma. It is the first link in the psychological chain leading to forgiveness. If you're unable to forgive him, your entire emotional system will become clogged with bitterness, resentment, and hostility.

In the fourth chapter of Ephesians, Paul taught the importance of expressing anger and the consequences if you don't. Read this verse: "Be angry, and yet do not sin; do not let the sun go down on your anger" (v. 26). The anger Paul described is obviously not sinful anger. It is not rage or hostility, but the anger that *precedes* rage and hostility. If you express this anger, it is released and you won't sin. And most important, it will keep you from giving Satan "an opportunity."

The anger noted in Ephesians 4:31 is an entirely different kind of anger: "Get rid of all bitterness, rage and anger, brawling and slander, along with every form of malice" (NIV). The terms in this verse refer to anger that is sinful and destructive: smoldering, held, in resentments and explosive, violent wrath.

I believe the apostle was saying that if you don't express your Ephesians 4:26 anger, you'll end up with Ephesians 4:31 anger. And that kind of anger breaks God's law and destroys you. It will also prevent you from experiencing Ephesians 4:32 (which immediately follows Paul's teaching about anger): "And be kind to one another, tender-hearted, forgiving each other, just as God in Christ also has forgiven you."

The third reason to get angry is that it gives you the ability to obey the Bible's instructions on how to confront your husband and his sin. The Matthew 18 road is going to be a very hard road. To follow my affair recovery program, you've got to be strong and tough. And to be strong and tough, you need to be angry.

Fourth, your anger helps motivate your husband to do the steps in my recovery program. You've lost his respect, and it's essential that you get it back as soon as you can. Once he respects you again, he can love you again. He won't work to get back a pitiful wimp who absorbed his deliberate, vicious, heartless treatment of her and took part of his blame. He won't work to get back someone who is willing to forgive without anger or hold him accountable for his sin. Why bother? Actually, he already can have you if he wants you. He just doesn't want you. I know that's hard to accept, but the facts tell me it's true.

The best thing for him is to rock back and forth in the blast of your righteous anger over his sin. He needs to see that you are furious. You are over him. You have had it. He may work to win back an angry, incredibly offended woman whom he has lost. The only option he is being offered is to work to win you back. This must be made so clear to him that he cannot miss it.

Peter, Jesus' disciple, was a dear friend of Jesus, one of His special three friends. Jesus never stopped loving Peter despite his sins and failings. Yet when confrontation was needed, Jesus rebuked Peter's behavior: "Get behind Me, Satan!" (Matt. 16:23). The Lord even asked Peter a hard, probing question—in fact, He asked the question three times (and that was after Peter's denial of Him): "Simon, son of John, do you love Me?" (John 21:15–17). How hard your husband works to win you back will reveal how much he loves you.

You need to follow Christ's example and confront a man whom you love very much. In fact, just like Jesus, you should confront him because you love him and want the best for him. You're asking the same question Jesus asked Peter: "Do you love me?" Your husband's behavior after the confrontation will answer this question.

Your sustained anger will cause your husband pain. And that pain can result in real change. The causal relationship between pain and change is a biblical concept. Paul, on purpose, hurt the Corinthian Christians with a tough letter (2 Cor. 7:8). But they needed to be hurt! Read about their response to Paul's hurtful letter: "Yet now I am happy, not because you were made sorry, but because your sorrow led you to repentance. For you became sorrowful as God intended and so were not harmed in any way by us. Godly sorrow brings repentance that leads to salvation and leaves no regret, but worldly sorrow brings death" (2 Cor. 7:9–10 NIV).

Do you see? Paul was happy he hurt those believers whom he loved (2 Cor. 2:4) because it caused godly sorrow, which, in turn, led them to repent. Repentance, here and throughout the Bible, means much more than feeling sorry for one's sins. It means a distinct, genuine *change*. This godly sorrow is exactly what you want to create in your husband.

How do you create godly sorrow and repentance in your husband? By being angry! Your anger keeps the crisis of his adultery at the forefront, the only issue that matters at the moment. You don't want to lessen or defuse the crisis by being only hurt and weak. Change—deep change—occurs only in a crisis. God wants you to stay angry with this intense but rational and coherent anger, and to keep the crisis at a fever pitch until your husband breaks and feels the awesome weight of godly sorrow.

Finally, your anger will help you rebuild your life if your husband does not repent and change. Anger is your friend in this terrible time. Your God-given friend. If there is a divorce, you've got to be strong and resilient "enough" to get through it with your sanity, your self-respect, and your self-esteem intact, and with your children intact. You're going to take a lot of hits from your husband, who wants desperately to lay blame on you and sidestep personal responsibility. You have a huge job to do and a million and one things to handle. Hurt, sadness, shock, confusion, and indecision won't help you. Anger will propel you to your new life whether that will be with your husband or not. Forcing yourself to get angry and stay angry will give you the kind of strength you need to survive this nightmare, attempt to save your marriage and family, and (if necessary) start over.

I paused and looked at my client. She wasn't crying anymore, and there was a new look—a look of determination (and maybe *hope*)—on her face. She said, "Okay. I think you're right. I think God wants me to get past the obstacles and get angry at my husband. Can you tell me how to do it?"

I smiled because I live for such moments in therapy. I responded, "Yes, I can. Helping adultery victims get angry and stay angry and accomplish what must be done is one of my specialties." Turn the page to find out what I told her to do.

SIX

FROM WELCOME MAT TO SLAMMING DOOR

How to Get Mad and Stay Mad

If you continue to lie down in front of your adulterous husband and act like a welcome mat, guess what he's going to do? He's going to keep wiping his feet on you. Wiping, wiping, wiping. Day after day. Week after week. Month after month. To save yourself from this humiliation and force your husband to respect you, you must go from the welcome mat to the slamming door. You must slam his fingers again and again in the door of your anger. Here's how you get angry enough to do it.

FOCUS ON THE NEGATIVE

Did you notice the title of this section? Not exactly the advice they give you in the average Christian living book, is it? I want you to know, I mean it.

Don't say any "I love you's" to him. He may say it to you (although I doubt it), but don't say it back to him. In fact, don't say anything nice to him at all. Who cares if he runs an errand for you, does a household chore, puts gas in your car, or shows he is "really trying"? Does this make up for his having intercourse with some morally degenerate female who doesn't mind destroying a marriage and family? No!

What you want is a broken and contrite heart. What you want are a million heartfelt apologies, full acceptance of the incredible damage he has done to you and his children, and his every effort at every moment to help your open wounds heal. What you want is a man who will continue following my affair recovery program in the face of your ongoing anger and disgust.

Don't get your hopes up if he suddenly decides he wants you back. Stay pulled back and very leery even if he starts saying and doing the right things. It's too soon to know what he's up to or whether he's sincere. Chances are very good, he's just schmoozing you, stalling for time, or easing what's left of his conscience. Do not rush back into his arms. Do not express your hurt and sadness to him. If you're that vulnerable and it turns out he really doesn't want you back, you'll be devastated again. The one last hope you are entertaining will be dashed. Maintain your position as the furious, uncompromising ice queen until he's well on his way to genuine, Holy Spirit–controlled change.

Always refer to the other woman as *the paramour* or *the prostitute*. Don't call her a lady because she's not one. Don't show any respect whatever for her. She's a home wrecker and a witch and a low-life slimeball. Call what he did adultery, not an affair. Don't call your husband by his first name, either. That's too personal and affectionate. Use *buster* or *you* or his last name. The colder and more impersonal you can be, the better.

Avoid going on a nostalgic tour down memory lane. It's a bad idea—a very bad idea. Don't look through your wedding album. Don't watch your wedding video. Don't look at old pictures of the two of you in happier days. I can just see you on the couch, clutching the tissue box, boo-hooing your way through memories of the good old days. He killed those memories when he engaged in those same intimate, loving behaviors with another woman. It's pathetic behavior, and it will make you depressed and weak.

VISUALIZE

One of the reasons you need to know everything about his affair (as I recommended in Chapter 3 and will recommend in Chapter 8) is that it is a powerful, effective way to tap your anger. There's pain in the details, and that pain will fuel your anger. I am not talking here about pitying yourself or hanging on to pain for no reason. The more you know about him and the adulteress, the angrier you'll be. Demand that he tell you what they talked about, what they did together, and the specific places they went. If he has the unbelievable nerve to refuse to tell you the details of his affair, this attempt to protect himself from (legitimate) feelings of guilt or embarrassment ought to make you even angrier.

No matter how painful, visualize the two of them together. Picture them talking at the office, at a restaurant, and in his car. Imagine them kissing in a parking lot. In your mind's eye see them having sex. Scripture is not vague when sexual sin is described. The apostle Paul didn't mince words when he bluntly told the Corinthian Christians about the man who was in an adulterous relationship with his mother—or stepmother (1 Cor. 5). The account of King David's adultery with Bathsheba is specific, detailed, and vivid (2 Sam. 11–12). A precise, step-by-step picture is painted of Amnon's rape of his half sister, Tamar (2 Sam. 13). When you read these graphic stories of sexual sin, you have a strong emotional reaction. I believe that's how God wants you to respond.

These pictures I'm asking you to put into your mind are terrible; nevertheless, they happened. They will energize your anger. You might even drive to one of the places you know the two of them visited. Just dropping by the locale of one of their trysts will make you see red.

One of my clients was having a hard time feeling angry at her unfaithful husband. Even though he'd just ended a six-month affair, he wouldn't tell her the details. That hurt her more than made her angry. I asked her what his favorite possessions were. Without hesitation she said, "His grandmother's china collection and his computer." Right there in my office and throughout the week I had her visualize herself throwing each piece of his precious china against the wall in their den, smashing it to bits. Then she was to picture herself sprinkling the jagged shards of the now worthless china all over his stupid computer. It was a powerful picture, and it stirred her anger. Even though there never could be any real comparison in value, making the connection between his sacred and precious vows to her and the china he loved wasn't lost on her. I instructed her to visualize this scene every time she was feeling hurt and weak or tending to minimize what he had done.

Identify the things your husband values the most—obviously, *you* were not even one of them—and create a scenario in your mind's eye of yourself trashing them. Maybe it's his golf clubs, his morning paper, his special coffee mug, an irreplaceable sculpture, the television set, his office, or his beautifully manicured lawn. Another client visualized beating her husband's midlife-crisis red sports car into a useless wreck with a sledgehammer. She actually laughed out loud at the point in her visualization when she smashed in the windshield.

Do the Top Ten

Rocky Glisson, my best friend and counseling associate, came up with a great idea we both use in helping victims get in touch with their anger. It's called the top ten. We ask the client to write down on a three-by-five card the top ten bad, painful things in his affair that her husband has done to her. She keeps this card with her at all times—in her blouse pocket, in her purse. When she's feeling weepy and hurt and needs a fresh burst of anger, she just whips out the top ten, and it reminds her of the rotten things he's done to her.

Here's one client's top ten:

1. He said he never loved me and shouldn't have married me.
2. He blamed me for his miserable, sinful adultery.
3. He betrayed me in the worst possible way.
4. He broke my kids' hearts.
5. He lied to me about his adultery for five solid months.
6. He put me at risk for AIDS and other sexually transmitted diseases.
7. He criticized my weight and appearance.
8. He spent our money on his prostitute.
9. He changed my whole life with his sinful choices.
10. His adultery has forced me to look for a job.

Doesn't reading this list make you mad for her? I'll bet you can identify with a number of these points, can't you? Make a top ten list that goes to the heart of what your husband has done to you, and it will galvanize your internal anger.

If your situation is grim, and it looks as though even my program isn't going to turn your husband around, there are two more lists you may write that will help you stay angry through the divorce process. These two sample lists were written by clients:

TEN REASONS WHY I AM BETTER OFF WITHOUT (NAME OF SPOUSE)

1. I don't have to live with constant rejection.
2. I don't have to wonder where he is when he's late.
3. I can grocery shop and buy things I like.
4. I have more room in the refrigerator.
5. I can cook and have people over for dinner.
6. My house stays much cleaner.
7. I can get back my joy, peace, and confidence.
8. I can buy a camera.
9. I can teach my kids how to live for Jesus without any interference from him.
10. I am now free to go to church whenever I want, leave the country on missions trips, and serve God in other ways.

FIVE THINGS I COULD DO WITH MY WEDDING RING

1. Destroy it.
2. Store it in the attic.
3. Trade it in on another piece of jewelry I like.
4. Have it melted down and shaped into a cross.
5. Exchange my diamonds for new ones and have them placed on the cross since God's love *is* forever.

STUPIDITY DEMANDS A RESPONSE

As if he has not hurt you enough, your adulterous husband is going to say more hurtful—but also a lot of incredibly stupid—things to you. It's important that you respond (and not *react*) to these damaging barbs with snappy, honest statements. If you just take his verbal hits, you'll sink into more hurt and depression. If you respond, you'll clear the pain out of your system and stay angry, assertive, and confident. Plus, you'll shake him up a little and gain some respect points. Don't get dragged into long, vicious arguments. They will serve no useful purpose. Just slip your blade in and out quickly, calmly, and rationally. Then walk away.

As a psychologist who has worked with couples for almost twenty years, I've discovered that all adulterous spouses tend to say the same stupid things. So I have developed a basic list of stupid comments and my tried-and-true, effective comebacks. It's kind of like *Cliffs Notes* for how to deal with the strange, twisted, denying language of adulterous spouses. After I give you a couple of paragraphs of instructions, I'll present my list. Read it and copy it into a notebook. Just writing the list will help stir your justifiable anger.

When you have your written copy of comments and responses, keep it close by because you'll have plenty of chances to use it. Adulterous spouses tend to repeat their stupid comments again and again. And unless you are following my plan, you will allow your spouse to brainwash you into believing them. There are a number of ways you can choose to respond to him. For example, you can reply verbally in person immediately after he cuts you with a comment. This is easier to do if you think quickly on your feet and remember the appropriate retort from my list.

Since it's often difficult to respond right away with a suitable statement, feel free to refer to your list. Run your finger down the selections right in front of him. Say something like, "Hmm, let's see. That was stupid comment number fifteen. Let me read you my response."

If you can't think of a response at the time or don't have your list handy (or need a break to compose yourself), it's fine to tell him you will reply later and get back to him when you are prepared. When you are ready and the time is right, say, "I have a response now to that stupid, painful remark you made to me this morning." Then lay it on him. Of course, some things he'll say won't be on my list, and you'll have to take some time to come up with a response. There's nothing wrong with a delayed response. It's better late than never.

It's perfectly okay to deliver your responses by phone or e-mail, or in a brief written note. If it's easier to express yourself from a distance and out of his presence, go ahead. It doesn't matter how you do it as long you do it.

Now that you have your instructions, here's my list:

EFFECTIVE RESPONSES TO STUPID STATEMENTS

STUPID COMMENT: I haven't been happy.

YOUR RESPONSE: Show me in the Bible where God promises happiness. Is it in the same section that states God's words, "Be holy, even as I am holy"?

STUPID COMMENT: You're not attractive to me anymore.

YOUR RESPONSE: You're not exactly Brad Pitt yourself.

STUPID COMMENT: We got married too young.

YOUR RESPONSE: Most people get married young. You can do better than that.

STUPID COMMENT: I shouldn't have married you.

YOUR RESPONSE: Funny, I don't recall having a gun to your head at the wedding.

STUPID COMMENT: I wasn't in the will of God when I married you.

YOUR RESPONSE: Maybe not, but after marriage, it's God's will that you stay married. Did you think your adultery was God's will?

STUPID COMMENT: I don't want to be married anymore.

YOUR RESPONSE: Yeah, I noticed. I can't believe I married a quitter.

STUPID COMMENT: I'm pleasing you, the kids, and our families, but I'm not pleasing me.

YOUR RESPONSE: Oh, what a shame! We all know the Bible teaches that we need to please ourselves. What was that Bible reference?

STUPID COMMENT: I think breaking up is best for the kids.

YOUR RESPONSE: Yeah, you're right. Having their self-esteem, confidence, and security destroyed will be good for them. Did you think your illicit relationship with this woman was also best for them?

STUPID COMMENT: I need some space.

YOUR RESPONSE: Look between your ears; there's plenty. Actually, I need space too. I won't beg you to stay. In fact, I think you need to go. Get your stuff together and leave as soon as you can.

STUPID COMMENT: I don't know who I am.

YOUR RESPONSE: I know who you are. You're an idiot. An idiot who's on the verge of losing his wife, his family, and his God because of his sinful choices.

STUPID COMMENT: I don't know what I want.

YOUR RESPONSE: Baloney. Based on your behavior, you know exactly what you want.

STUPID COMMENT: We've drifted apart.

YOUR RESPONSE: No, we didn't. You moved.

STUPID COMMENT: If you'd met my needs, I wouldn't have had the affair.

YOUR RESPONSE: Don't ever blame me for your adultery. It was 100 percent your fault.

STUPID COMMENT: I know what I'm doing isn't biblical, but I don't care.

YOUR RESPONSE: Well, God cares. Read, for example, 1 Thessalonians 4 or 1 Corinthians 6. I wouldn't want to be in your shoes right about now.

STUPID COMMENT: Let's have an amicable divorce so we can still be friends.

YOUR RESPONSE: Help me here. If we're friends, why are you divorcing me? If you are a friend, why did you do what you did to me? You're no friend of mine. You're my enemy. You've hurt me and the children as few enemies would ever hurt us.

STUPID COMMENT: We weren't really married.

YOUR RESPONSE: Wow! We weren't married? Thanks for telling me. I could have sworn we were married all those years. It must have been a bad dream.

STUPID COMMENT: I've wanted out for years, but I've hung in there until now.

YOUR RESPONSE: God says you're supposed to hang in there until you're dead. You're checking out a little early.

ALTERNATE RESPONSE: So, for all those years you said nothing. What dishonesty!

STUPID COMMENT: This is so hard for me.

YOUR RESPONSE: Oh, stop playing the poor martyr. Sin is always hard on a person. Its wages are legitimately *earned*.

STUPID COMMENT: I love this other woman.

YOUR RESPONSE: No, you don't. You don't know what love is. Tell the truth: you lust for her.

STUPID COMMENT: I feel sorry for [name of paramour]. I don't want to hurt her.

YOUR RESPONSE: She made her bed. Now she can lie in it. Adultery has its consequences. Destroying a home and a family should bring sorrow. Let someone else help her pick up the pieces.

STUPID COMMENT: God has released me from this marriage.

YOUR RESPONSE: What Bible are you reading? No, Satan has "released" you from this marriage. Look, if anyone has a marriage release from God, it's me.

STUPID COMMENT: I never meant to hurt you.

YOUR RESPONSE: No, that's a lie. You knew how much you would hurt me, and you succeeded.

STUPID COMMENT: I don't want to hurt you anymore.

YOUR RESPONSE: Believe me, you won't. It's your turn to hurt, and God will see to it.

STUPID COMMENT: I need time.

YOUR RESPONSE: You don't need time. You need a brain. On second thought, maybe you do need time to find God and to repent. And to find your brain.

STUPID COMMENT: I said I was sorry.

YOUR RESPONSE: Sorry is not good enough. I want change. I want a brand-new husband.

STUPID COMMENT: You're crazy, hysterical, paranoid, out of control, too worked up, vengeful . . .

YOUR RESPONSE: You wonder why I'm upset, bonehead? If *I'd* committed adultery, you'd be pretty upset yourself. You'd be insanely angry, disgusted, shamed. I'm not apologizing for my feelings.

STUPID COMMENT: I'm witnessing to this lady.

YOUR RESPONSE: Well, Mr. Missionary, read Proverbs 5 carefully, and then tell me how God feels about what you're doing. You're not witnessing to her. You're sinning with her!

STUPID COMMENT: It's not you; it's me.

YOUR RESPONSE: That's the one thing you've said that is correct. It is you. It's all you. You have serious problems, Mr. Dysfunctional!

STUPID COMMENT: I don't love you anymore.

YOUR RESPONSE: I don't love you anymore, either. I loved my old husband but not this one.

RECRUIT ANGER COACHES

You won't be able to get angry and stay angry all by yourself. You will need support and encouragement, and you will need to be accountable to another. Recruit a small core group of friends and family to help keep you angry. Avoid the namby-pamby, weak-kneed, spineless souls who want you to lie down in front of your husband's Mack truck. Let them ruin someone else's life and marriage.

Sign up on your team individuals who are furious with your husband and his behavior. Ask these persons to monitor you closely for signs of weakness, passivity, and depression. Ask them to ride you and make sure you're not cutting your husband any slack he hasn't earned with sincere, hard work. Ask them to listen to you vent, and ask them to rally to your side. Ask them to confront your husband when necessary. Ask them to tell you the truth, even when it stings. These are Proverbs 27:5–6 friends:

> Better is open rebuke
> Than love that is concealed.
> Faithful are the wounds of a friend.

BE PHYSICALLY ACTIVE

A regular, vigorous exercise regimen is an absolute must when you're living this kind of nightmare. Doctor-approved, appropriate exercise is a great way to release your stress and express your anger as well as lift your spirits. The clients I've seen who choose to be out-of-shape couch potatoes and don't like to sweat have tremendous difficulty getting angry and standing up to an adulterous spouse. They tend to meekly sink deeper into their couches. Exercise can help give you the energy, strength, confidence, stamina, and anger to carry out my difficult program of counterattack.

FAKE IT 'TIL YOU MAKE IT

Even when you're following my anger-inducing steps, it still might take a while to get angry. Before you actually feel your anger, you'll need to fake it. Pretend. Act as if you're furious with your husband. Every hour, every day, is critical after you find out your husband has been or still is in an adulterous relationship. You can't afford to waste time waiting for your anger to catch up with you. As a good friend of mine used to say, "Fake it 'til you make it."

Your husband needs to believe you're angry even if you're not. The fact is, you are angry in there somewhere! Acting angry may even trigger the real anger buried inside. If you can't do anything else, at least pull way back from him. Go into shunning mode. Ignore him. Say nothing to him. He'll interpret this behavior as anger, and that'll be good enough until the real McCoy kicks in.

Are you wondering how things turned out for the female client whose story I began telling in Chapter 5? I'll give you the short version. With God's help and my instructions, she got angry. And she stayed angry long enough to carry out the other elements of my anti-adultery program. She acquired fresh strength, she began to move on with her life, she was able to protect the children, and she was able to fight back against her husband and his sin.

It was touch and go with her husband for a good three or four weeks. She had kicked him out of the home and was prepared *to live without him.* But he came around! He repented and worked hard to help her heal, and he became a new man and husband. They have a great marriage today. Her ability to get angry when she needed to is one of the main reasons why.

Now that you understand the importance of anger, you're ready to launch into the heart of my recovery from adultery program. You will require your spouse to perform a series of specific actions if he wants to have a chance to stay married to you. He'll do them all without questioning. Without grumbling. Without any guarantee he'll be able to win you back.

There will be no compromises. No deals. He'll do what you demand, your way, and in your time frame. Period. Or he'll face serious consequences.

In the following chapters I'll take you through my program step-by-step. I want you to know exactly what to do. Then, I'll show you how my approach is supported by the Bible.

Even if your husband is not having an affair, I want you to read my recovery from adultery program (Chapters 7 through 12). He's still sinning, and you're going to follow many of the same steps in dealing with him. Then, after Chapter 12, skip to Chapter 15 for specific guidance on to what to do with a husband who's not in an affair but still does not love you.

SEVEN

"STOP YOUR ADULTERY—RIGHT NOW!"

How to End the Affair and Make Sure It's Over

You are furious. You are as cold as an Arctic winter. You are hard. You are mean. You are determined. You have turned the tables on your adulterous spouse. Until now, you've been in a panic over losing him. Now, he has lost you, and he'll have to work harder than he has ever worked in his life to win you back. It has probably taken you a few weeks or even a few months to get to this aggressive, tough love position. That's okay. You're here now, and you're ready to rumble.

You look him dead in the eye and tell him if he has any hope of salvaging his marriage and family, he will end his adultery immediately. Not tomorrow. Not next week. Right away. It's either you or his paramour, and he'd better make up his mind on the spot. You will not tolerate the continuation of this disgraceful, destructive, and sinful relationship for even one more minute.

If his response is anything less than an unqualified, heartfelt, "Yes, ma'am, it's over," tell him to get out of your home. Right then, no matter what time it is. If he refuses to leave, go into the shunning mode. (I'll explain shunning and separation in detail in later chapters.) He just dug his hole deeper and will now have to work even harder before you'll talk to him again. In fact if he balks at any step in my program, you'll shift into shunning and separation mode.

ATTITUDE IS EVERYTHING

Ending the sinful liaison is only the beginning. He must be genuinely sorry for what he has done. I mean, really sorry. I mean, almost unbelievably, deeply, and agonizingly sorry. In this case attitude is everything. We're talking true brokenness. True remorse. True, life-changing repentance. You want the same reaction that King David expressed when the prophet Nathan nailed the king's heart to the wall with God's message about his adultery with Bathsheba: "You are the man!" (2 Sam. 12:7). Nathan described the enormity of David's sin with pungent words: "Why have you despised the word of the LORD by doing evil in His sight?" (2 Sam. 12:9). David's words in Psalm 51:17 reveal his complete brokenness and sorrow:

> The sacrifices of God are a broken spirit;
> A broken and contrite heart, O God,
>   Thou wilt not despise.

Read Psalm 51, where David recorded his powerful, personal description of his response to his sin of adultery. Ask your husband to read it aloud to you. David confessed his sin (v. 1). He admitted he sinned against God (v. 4) and humbly asked for forgiveness (v. 2). He begged God to restore their close fellowship (vv. 11–12). He said his heart was both broken and contrite (v. 17). If your husband's response to his sin is anything other than David's response, he's not where he needs to be. He is further insulting you and God. Go into shunning and separation mode.

The story of Nathan and David is one more biblical example of the tough, harsh, unyielding approach you need to take with your unfaithful spouse. It's the same approach Jesus took with the hypocritical, sinful Pharisees. Matthew 23:27 records these brutal words of Jesus: "Woe to you, scribes and Pharisees, hypocrites! For you are like whitewashed tombs which on the outside appear beautiful, but inside they are full of dead men's bones and all uncleanness."

It's the same approach the apostle Paul took with the sexually immoral Corinthian church members. Paul told the Corinthians he had given the immoral man to Satan (1 Cor. 5:5) and commanded them to "remove the wicked man from among yourselves" (1 Cor. 5:13). It's the same approach God always wants us to use when confronting people in serious sin.

"It's All My Fault"

He admits the affair is 100 percent his fault. He makes no more excuses. He offers no more rationalizations. He offers no more of the stupid comments I covered in Chapter 6. He does not blame you in any way for his affair. He acknowledges that the whole flimsy, sin-encrusted defense justifying his adultery is a pack of lies and a complete cover-up. He agrees to contact all the persons he lied to about the affair and, in your hearing (in person or on the phone), tell them the truth.

He faces his sin directly and calls it what it is: adultery. He stops all his efforts toward damage control and minimizing what he's done with statements like these: "We were just really good friends." "It lasted only a month." "We only went to lunch a few times." "I was under pressure, and she was a good listener." "I communicated with her only on the Internet, and I never was with her in person." "We never had sex, so it was not an affair." Such stupid statements end, and before God and you, he agrees he had a full-blown, absolutely sinful, as-bad-as-it-can-be adulterous affair. He says, "It was adultery, it was all my fault, and I'll do anything to help you heal and win you back." You reply, "We'll see." And you continue your list of behaviors he has to do.

THE FINAL PHONE CALL

Telling you his affair is over isn't good enough. Your husband's a liar, and you can't trust him yet. As soon as possible, he will place a phone call to his "lover." (Of course, he will have told you her name and everything about her and their relationship—more about this in the next chapter.) You'll listen on the extension.

In a cold, firm voice, here's what he'll say:

This is the last time I'll talk to you in person or on the telephone. Listen closely. Our relationship was sinful, I'm ashamed of it, and now it's over. I don't love you. I never did. Though I showed the opposite, I love my wife, and I'm going to work on our marriage. She's with me now and listening to this call. Never contact me in any way ever again. Leave me and my family alone.

After delivering this message, he'll hang up abruptly. This is the best way for an affair to end—in a nasty, brutal, miserable way. He needs to reject her in this call. We want this woman to feel bad—very bad—and to go away. She can have an affair with some other fool, but her affair with your fool is over.

I don't care if he tells you his affair has been over for months. Who believes him? Even if it is true, *how* an affair ends is important.

It needs to end badly. A final lunch in their special booth at their favorite restaurant, sex one last time at her place, or a tearful good-bye in a motel parking lot won't get the job done. These aren't good-byes. They're hellos! These touching scenes further cement his "feelings" for the woman in his sinful, mixed-up heart. In his twisted mind they may even legitimize what they have been doing. Demand that he make this phone call.

If he can't reach the woman by telephone fairly quickly, he can write a letter with the same rejecting message. He *won't* write "Dear _____" because she's not dear to him and never should have been. It'll be just her first name on the opening line, the body of the letter, and his first name as the last line. He'll type it because that makes it even more impersonal. You'll read it, you'll watch him put it in an envelope, together you'll walk to a United States mailbox, and he'll drop it in.

Speaking of phone calls, please don't call the paramour. Don't sink to her level. Don't beg her to stop seeing your husband. Doing this strips away your pride and dignity. And if the affair isn't over yet, the first person she'll call after hanging up with you is your husband. They'll have a good laugh over your desperate pleas. Don't call to express your anger and disgust with her. Frankly, she's not worth it, and you'll feel humiliated and dirty afterward. If you have already talked to her, it's not the end of the world. Just don't do it again.

No Contact Ever Again

He'll agree to never again have any contact with this person—for *any* reason. He won't talk on the phone with her. He won't see her in person. He won't read any letters she might send. He will not read or respond to her e-mails. If she attempts to contact him, he'll utterly reject her and report the attempted contact to you. If she calls him, he will hang up. If she says hello in person, he will not respond, even with a word or gesture.

If he and his paramour work at the same company, one of them has to leave. If she won't quit, he will. The only possible exception is in a huge company where they literally will not ever see each other—entering and leaving, on the elevator, in the parking lot, wherever. Even then, it's up to you as the offended party to make this decision. If you can't tolerate his working in the same building with this woman (and I wouldn't blame you), he has to look for another job immediately.

ALL CONNECTIONS SEVERED

Every single link to the other woman must be eliminated. He'll throw out any letters, cards, and gifts given to him by her. In fact, you'll destroy all these items together. If they had sex in a car, that car will be sold or traded. If they had sex in your home, it's usually a good idea to sell it and move. If they had sex in your bed, at the very least you'll buy a new bed and an entirely new set of bed linens and bedroom furniture. If this woman is a neighbor, you will definitely sell your home and get out of there. If she attends the same church as you and your husband, either she leaves and finds a new church, or the two of you do.

Because trust is zero and it comes back slowly, you'll need to keep checking on him to make sure he's not having any further contact with the paramour. For at least several months following the end of the affair, you'll be in detective mode. With his full and unquestioned permission, you'll check the calls he has made from home and his cell phone. You'll check the computer for e-mails. He will account for every single minute of every day, and he won't complain or mind doing it.

You'll be able to call him anytime on his cell phone (if he

doesn't have one, he gets one) and ask what he's doing, where he is now, where he has been, what his plans are for the rest of the day, and any other questions you feel like asking. He'll get a new cell phone number. Every day, probably more than once a day, you'll ask him if he has had any contact with her. He'd better have the right answer, and he'd better be as gracious and humble as any man could ever be when he answers.

No More Feelings

It is very common, particularly with a longer affair, for your spouse to continue to have feelings of "love" and "caring" for his partner in adultery. It is also completely unacceptable and a vicious insult to you. These feelings mean five things, all bad:

1. The affair is continuing, at least in his mind and emotions.

2. The adulteress is still in his heart; you are not.

3. He is much more likely—obviously—to have ongoing contact with her.

4. He is still justifying his sin and is refusing to deal directly with it.

5. Satan still has him by the throat.

Your husband will say things along these lines: "She is the only person who really understands me." "We were soul mates." "She's the only person with whom I could ever truly be myself." "Our relationship was perfect." He may or may not add, "Our sex was great too." "Our relationship also was a spiritual one." This last statement he may offer as the pièce de résistance of his efforts at justification. These are outrageous and—with the possible exception of the great sex claim—totally false statements and need to be confronted immediately and aggressively.

You see how subtle and effective Satan is? He knows your husband's weaknesses, his desires, and his resentments toward you. Satan has matched him up with someone who *seems* to be a soul mate. Who *seems* to understand him and meet all of his needs. And it feels fantastic! But it's all a deceptive fantasy, and when his life is destroyed, Satan will be laughing the loudest.

If your husband makes any statement indicating he still has feelings for the paramour, you need to do four things as quickly as you can. First, throw up in the bucket you keep handy when you're talking to him. Second, blast him verbally with your righteous anger and disgust. Third, tell him to read chapters 5, 6, and 7 of the book of Proverbs to find out how he'll end up. Fourth, tell him he can go to her if he wants. Then move into shunning and separation mode.

This affair is not over, and the healing of your marriage has not begun until he is repulsed by his paramour and crazy in love with you. He ends his affair not because of an obligation. Not because of the kids. Not because it's the right thing to do (even though it is). Not because he has to. He ends his adulterous affair because he *wants* to and makes the choice of his own free will. He's not confused anymore. He knows what he wants. You! He knows who he really loves and wants to win back. You! His behavior, his attitude, his words, and your intuition all tell you that the adulteress is out of his heart and you are back in.

AIDS AND STD TESTING

He will immediately schedule a test for the human immunodeficiency virus (HIV) and tests for the major sexually transmitted diseases: herpes, gonorrhea, and others. Because of his reckless sexual behavior, he has put you at risk for these diseases. Plus, this testing brings home to him the enormity of his sin. He will be tested right away and again in six months. You'll have to be tested, too, but he'll be tested first. And make sure he brings you written results of these tests. His word isn't worth much yet.

COUNSELING

He will attend therapy, along with you, with the counselor of *your* choice. Find the best Christian professional therapist in your area. Your marriage is at stake, and you must see the right person. Get a list from your pastor, Focus on the Family, and friends.

Call each therapist, and ask a series of specific questions. You want a solid Christian, someone who has a personal relationship with Jesus Christ and regularly attends a local church. You want someone with years of experience working with married couples who have had to deal with one partner's adultery. You want a therapist who is tough on the perpetrator of the affair and will follow my program. Explain to him or her the basic parts of my book and say this is the approach you want to use. If the therapist disagrees and advocates a wimpy, nonbiblical approach, say thank you and keep calling.

In therapy your husband will agree to take a searching look at his life, his family background, his personality, any unresolved issues, and his weaknesses. If he is a sex addict, he'll address this disorder in both group and individual psychotherapy. With his life in pieces because of his affair, there is no better time than now for him to work hard to change: as an individual, a husband, and a father.

SPIRITUAL GROWTH AND ACCOUNTABILITY

He will tell your pastor about his affair—all of it, and with you present—and agree to follow an intensive spiritual growth program.

Whatever your pastor sets up for him, he'll do: personal Bible study, men's small group, discipleship program. Your husband will give permission for your pastor and any other men working with him to give you updates on his spiritual progress. Of course, he'll be sharing with you frequently how he's growing in his relationship with the Lord. When restoration has taken place to your satisfaction, I urge you both to read and follow my plan for spiritual intimacy in marriage in my book *A Marriage After God's Own Heart* (Multnomah).

Without God he can't stop the affair. Without God he can't get rid of his feelings for this woman. Without God he can't help you heal. Without God he can't truly change and become the man and husband and father he needs to be. With God he can do all these things. In the New Testament Jesus explained to His disciples that only God can perform the impossible feat of bringing a person into His kingdom: "Jesus looked at them intently, then said, 'Without God, it is utterly impossible. But with God everything is possible'" (Mark 10:27 TLB).

As soon as humanly possible, he will find a godly man who will be his accountability partner, mentor, and guide. Don't bother with nice, passive guys. This guy needs to be tough and blunt. Someone who will ask direct, specific, piercing questions and have a fit if they're not answered totally, honestly, and correctly. Your husband will tell this man, the selection of whom you will approve, everything about his affair. He'll tell the whole sordid story with you listening. He'll call this man at least once a week to report on how he's doing in ending the affair and helping you heal. He will give you permission to call this man to check on his progress. He'll be accountable, both spiritually and sexually, to at least one godly man for the rest of his life.

He will go to church with you. If you ask him to go to Sunday school and to a Bible study, he'll go. If you ask him to have a quiet time and read the Bible every day, he'll consent to this. If you ask him to attend a Promise Keepers event, he'll go. If you ask him to go to a marriage enrichment seminar with you, he'll go. If you ask him to read a book on marriage (such as this one) with you, he'll do it and in record time. If you ask him to watch a video series on marriage (such as one of mine) with you, he'll agree and do it without hesitation. By the way, go ahead and ask him to do all these things. They're all good for him, and his response will be a test of his commitment to you.

Even if your husband has stopped his adultery, has a great attitude, or seems to be developing one; even if he seems to be genuinely broken and repentant and follows through in all these initial areas, be wary. Do not indicate forgiveness too easily or too quickly. Stay pulled back, and keep your heart away from him. It's far too soon to tell if he's going to make all the changes he needs to make. You're in a marathon, and he has covered only the first one hundred yards. He has a long way to go.

EIGHT

THE TRUTH, THE WHOLE TRUTH, AND NOTHING BUT THE TRUTH

You Will Be Told Everything—
in Spoken Words and in Writing

Your husband has stopped his adulterous affair. He is showing that he respects you and that he wants to win you back. He seems genuinely broken and has taken *all* the critical, initial steps outlined in the previous chapter. So far, so good. Now you'll find out whether he's actually serious about his commitment to God and to you because now you demand that he tell you the truth about his affair. It will be the whole truth and nothing but the truth. As Nathan repeated each aspect of David's sin to David (and, by the way, the consequences that would follow), your husband must do the same to you regarding his sin.

Here is a small part of what Nathan told David:

> Why have you despised the word of the LORD by doing evil in His sight? You have struck down Uriah the Hittite with the sword, have taken his wife to be your wife, and have killed him with the sword of the sons of Ammon . . . Thus says the LORD, "Behold, I will raise up evil against you from your own household; I will even take your wives before your eyes, and give them to your companion, and he shall lie with your wives in broad daylight." (2 Sam. 12:9, 11)

THE HEALING IS IN THE DETAILS

You need to know the entire sordid, disgusting, sinful story of his relationship with this woman. All of it. He'll verbally tell you every possible detail he can remember. He will hold nothing back.

He'll begin with who she is and how they met. He'll continue with a day-by-day, week-by-week account of how the relationship developed: what he liked about her, exactly what they talked about, the type of communication they had (in person, e-mail and Internet, and telephone) and how often they communicated, the places they went, the promises they made to each other, the feelings he thought he had for her, the feelings she expressed for him, any future plans they had made, her personality and background, the names of other persons they spent time with as a couple, and anything else that will help you get a clear picture of the content and style of their relationship.

The one area in which you don't need to know specifics is the physical part of their relationship. He will tell you what they did physically in a general way, but not the gory details:

- "We held hands walking in the mall that Saturday afternoon."
- "We kissed in her car for about thirty minutes."
- "We kissed and fondled each other for twenty minutes on my office couch."
- "We kissed and did mutual masturbation with our clothes on in the motel room."
- "We had oral sex at her apartment that night."
- "We had intercourse fifteen times—five times in my car, ten times at her place."

It's important for you to know what they did physically, where they did it, and how often they did it. Their physical relationship is part of the story. He needs to tell you about it so he can fully confess his sin. You need to know so you can have a complete picture of his sinful relationship. When you know it all, then you can fully heal.

But you don't need to know exactly what their physical touching was like and how they performed the sexual actions. Don't ask what they did in foreplay. Don't ask what the intercourse was like. Don't ask if she had orgasms. Don't ask which positions they used. Don't ask what they talked about during intercourse. Don't ask for a description of her body or what he thought about it. Knowing these intimate details will cause you unnecessary distress and further complicate your sexual readjustment to your husband.

Many—in fact, the majority of—pastors and Christian authors and counselors believe strongly that focusing on the details of an affair is a mistake. They sincerely believe getting the whole truth out about the adultery and discussing it again and again is just too painful and will damage the marriage even further, to the point where it is beyond repair. They want you to pray about his "mistake," forgive, talk about the mistakes each of you made in the marriage that led to his sin, and move past that nasty old affair just as soon as you can. "Don't dredge up this horrible mess; it's past," they will tell you. It's as if by ignoring it, you could forget it. You have already imagined and had nightmares about what you *think* happened.

These well-meaning helpers couldn't be more wrong. Their approach is unsound not only psychologically and relationally, but biblically as well. The Bible teaches open, honest, verbal confession of sin (Matt. 3:6; Mark 1:5; Acts 19:18). The Bible teaches us to confess our sins directly to each other (Matt. 5:23–24; James 5:16).

When the Bible describes sinful behavior, the writers often go into detail. The story of David's sin with Bathsheba (2 Sam. 11–12) and his confession of that sin (Ps. 51) is told in detail. Why? Because the details are important.

The details are an essential part of the recovery process. The two of you and your marriage won't heal without them. How can your fallen husband be truly broken and truly change without a full and open and honest confession of his sin? If any of his sin stays inside, secret and unconfessed, it will slowly destroy him and your relationship. He'll be separated from God and from you by that unconfessed sin. He will not be broken. He will not repent. He will not change. What he will do is leave the door of his life open to Satan. And Satan will come in and do terrible, ongoing damage. He must confess directly to you because you are the one he harmed the most.

How can he gain a clear understanding of his sin and why he did it without directly facing every detail of his adultery? What were his motivations to look outside the marriage? What needs did he want to get met? What family of origin issues, past unresolved painful events, current stressors, personality weaknesses, and poor choices combined to create his adultery? Specifically, how did he allow Satan room to operate? He must find the answers to these questions, or he won't break the power of this sin in his life. He'll be very likely to have another affair or sin in some other, grievous way. The answers are in the details.

The details are important to your recovery too. How can you trust him without knowing exactly what he has done with the adulteress? You must have the answers to the questions in the previous paragraph, or you will never be able to trust him completely ever again. You'll always wonder if he'll do it again. And that's a terrible way to live. Without trust there is no respect.

Without trust and respect there is no genuine vulnerability, love, and intimacy.

How can you completely forgive him if you don't know completely what he's done? You can't forgive what you don't know. You can forgive him only for the specific, confessed sins he committed during the adulterous relationship. Issuing some blanket, general forgiveness for the kind of sins involved in the adultery without knowing exactly what those sins are is no more than a feeble attempt to deny reality and, however understandable, avoid pain. This kind of forgiveness is weak, passive, and unbiblical. It will prevent you and him from reaching true healing and reconciliation. Also, he can hide a great deal of what he has done when he uses only generalities.

How can you heal emotionally without confronting and reacting to all the sinful behaviors involved in the adultery? You can't! Your pain will remain inside you and eat away at you. The pain will be as great or greater if you must imagine what he did, for what is imagined may be worse than what really happened. You heal psychologically from painful events by reliving those events piece by piece, frame by frame, and expressing your emotions and thoughts about them. This is a fundamental, God-created law of trauma recovery. Most people, including the well-meaning helpers I mentioned, don't know this law. It is a recognized principle in the professions of psychology and psychiatry. It is the same process I use in therapy to help clients heal from every kind of trauma.

THE DOCUMENT

Your husband verbally expressing to you the nature of his adultery is important. He'll begin verbally sharing details right after the affair is discovered (and ended) and continue with verbal descriptions of his sinful relationship all the way through the recovery process. He'll answer *all* your questions about his affair with patience, gentleness, kindness, and humility. Or, he'll face your righteous wrath.

But just sharing verbally isn't enough. A crucial piece of my recovery program is the requirement that the adulterer write out, *in a letter to you,* the entire story of the affair. I call this the Document.

I instruct the adulterer to put down on paper the most painstakingly researched, detailed, and descriptive account of his affair that he can produce. I tell him to cover all the areas mentioned earlier in this chapter: who she is, how they met, what he liked about her, exactly what they talked about. The one exception—as in the couple's verbal discussions—is the specific details of their physical/sexual relationship.

I tell him in session, with his wife listening, to go back in time and relive the affair. To go over and over it in his mind. To rack his brain for information: dates, times, places, conversations. I ask him to pray that God will give him the memories he needs to put into the letter. I emphasize the more details, the better. He should not sidestep painful events, attempt damage control, or gloss over. In black and white he should put down all he can remember. If in doubt, he should write more, not less.

He is to include, in the same detailed way, every other affair and inappropriate relationship he has had during the course of his marriage. If pornography has been a problem, he should write a section covering the entire story of his mistakes in this area, including his first exposure and how the addiction developed. I warn him that if he does not include other women who should be in the Document, or omits any important infractions, he is continuing to lie. And he is seriously jeopardizing any hope of saving his marriage.

Your husband can't remember every single detail of his affair (or affairs). No one has a memory that good. But with God's help and his own tremendous effort, he can get 85 to 90 percent of the important, major information right. That's good enough. Your intense questioning will take care of the remaining 10 to 15 percent.

I usually give the adulterous spouse one week to complete the Document. He writes the letter in private. His spouse does not look as he works on it. Then, he brings it in and *reads* it to his spouse in a session with me. If you choose not to use a therapist, have your spouse read the Document to you in your home. Make sure no one is in the home as he reads it. After the reading, he hands it to his wife. She'll keep it—rereading it and asking questions based on it—for as long as she needs to. This might be a matter of weeks or months.

It's hard to find words to describe therapy sessions in which the Document is read. *Powerful. Agonizing. Painful. Humiliating. Unbelievably intense. Gut-wrenching. Brutal.* All these words apply, but so does the one word that is the point of the process: *healing.* (And let it never, ever, be forgotten: this experience is *nothing* compared to the powerful, agonizing, painful, humiliating, unbelievably intense, gut-wrenching, brutal, and heartbreaking experience the adultery caused his wife.)

Here are the reasons for, and the benefits of, preparing the Document:

It Gets All the Truth Out

It's vital that the complete story of the adultery come out as quickly as possible. When the adulterer is only talking about his affair, it's very easy (and common) for him to conceal, or omit, the extent of his sin. When the couple's discussions are only verbal, the truth tends to come out in spurts:

- "I didn't have an affair."
- "Well, all right, I did."
- "It was only emotional, not physical."
- "Okay, we kissed."
- "We tried to have sex, but I couldn't perform."
- "We had sex two times . . . no, three times."
- "It was safe sex."
- "No, it wasn't safe sex every time."

This kind of stalling and lying does serious damage. You'll feel as though you have to ask the right questions or you won't find out what really happened. You'll wonder whether you're getting the whole story and whether you're getting the truth.

Having to write down the affair forces the adulterer to think about exactly what happened and the sequence of events. He will share much more truth and much more detail in writing than he ever will verbally. And he'll do it more quickly.

It Limits and Contains the Trauma

Adultery hits your home like an unexpected tornado and suddenly rips it to pieces. You are surrounded by chaos and confusion. It is overwhelming. The Document gives the affair both form and limits. It helps you move past shock and denial, assess the extent of the damage, and get into recovery mode.

The Document provides you with a clear, contained picture of the adultery. You begin to get your hands around it. There's a beginning, a middle, and an end to the story. You don't have to wonder how bad it is and waste precious energy desperately trying to find out. With the affair on paper, it goes from an out-of-control, mysterious monster to a defined, manageable monster.

You'll know how bad it is, and you can expend energy working to heal from it.

It Creates Brokenness

The writing of his adulterous relationship cuts through your husband's thick wall of denial and deceit like a sharp sword. The power of his written sin forces him to face the horrible reality of his behavior and the incredible devastation it caused. He won't be able to apply damage-control tactics. Or to spin it. Or to ignore it. God will use the words, the sentences, and the paragraphs to create brokenness. And from brokenness can come repentance, which is making a 180-degree turn, undertaking a total change, and shaping a new, spiritual way of life.

It Creates Empathy

Your spouse's heart, terribly cold to you until now, will melt as he reads the Document to you. When he sees and hears your hurt and anguish and devastation, he'll realize what he has done to you. He'll never forget the look on your face. The deep woundedness in your eyes. He'll feel, maybe for the first time in your marriage, your pain. He'll connect to you emotionally. He'll work to ease your pain and help you heal from what he did to you.

It Kills His Feelings for the Paramour

Satan wants the adultery to end your marriage, but he'll certainly settle for your husband staying with you and pining away for his agony-causing, home-destroying paramour. The emotional tie between the adulterous partners must be broken. The Document can help do this job.

The other woman remains in his heart because of all the secrets they shared in their relationship: all the "deep" conversations, their rendezvous, and the things they did. When he writes all these secrets in his Document, he'll see them for what they really are: cheap, tacky, sleazy, sinful, and revolting. When what they did in private is exposed in the light of his Document, he won't think it's special any longer. He won't think or feel that she's special any longer. He'll see that what they had was a rotting piece of garbage that needs to be thrown out. He'll turn away from her in disgust and shame.

It Is Effective Punishment

I openly admit, without apology, that the Document is also punishment. Brutal, harsh, and humiliating punishment. It is the psychological equivalent of placing his hand firmly on a burning stove top and keeping it there for one full minute. He will remember the writing and reading of the Document for the rest of his life. I want, and I believe God wants, his affair always to be associated with a memory of terrible, searing pain. Reread 2 Samuel 12. The Lord forgave David after he repented of his adultery, but He still applied devastating punishment: murder would always haunt David's family, family members would rebel against him, his wives would be given to another man in full view of everyone, and his first child with Bathsheba would die.

Pain is a great motivator and sends a clear message: don't do it again. If this man repents and builds his relationship with God, and wonderful fellowship with Him is restored, he will be eternally thankful.

Punishment is a biblical concept. In Deuteronomy 28:20–57 we're taught that punishment follows the breaking of a covenant. God punishes us when we sin, so we will learn from our mistakes, turn from our sin, and be restored in relationship with Him and others. Your husband has broken his marriage covenant, and punishment will be part of what drives him to renew it. God is a very gracious God, but He is also the Judge. When we sin, He always provides consequences (Gen. 4:13).

It Is a Test of His Commitment and Love

Saying he's committed to you, loves you, and will do anything to win you back is nice. It's also easy and most often is meaningless. Action counts. Writing the Document is an extremely difficult and painful task. It demands tremendous effort, honesty, vulnerability, and a recognition and acknowledgment of his sin (1 John 1:9). It will be the hardest thing he has ever done in his life. *If he refuses to do it, you know he doesn't love you and is not yet worthy of you or your time and attention.* If he agrees to do it, you know he's serious about working to restore your marriage. You'll still stay pulled back and careful, but it's a step in the right direction.

HOW DOES HE REACT TO THE DOCUMENT?

I always give the Document assignment to the adulterer in the presence of the person's victim. I want her—I want you—to see his initial reaction. The way he responds to the Document gives you a very accurate read on the true condition of his heart and mind. I've included some typical, classic responses to the Document and my respective comebacks:

CLASSIC RESPONSE: I am shocked that you'd even ask me to write down my affair!

MY COMEBACK: You're probably not a tiny fraction as shocked as your wife was when she found out about your adultery!

CLASSIC RESPONSE: I'm angry, furious, outraged about this . . . this . . . Document thing.

MY COMEBACK: What right do you have to be angry? You've got nerve, I'll give you that. I wish you were this angry at yourself for what you've done. After what you have done before God, to your wife and your family, you are angry because you are asked to describe your behavior—behavior you chose deliberately to engage in?

CLASSIC RESPONSE: This isn't fair to _____ [his paramour].

MY COMEBACK: What? You're still protecting her? She knew you were married and the adultery would break your wife's heart and demolish your family. If you want to protect her, go to her now.

CLASSIC RESPONSE: I'm afraid the Document will hurt my wife terribly and push her away.

MY COMEBACK: You've already hurt her enough to last two lifetimes. There's a risk you'll lose her for good, but it's a risk worth taking. If you don't do it, you'll lose her for sure. You have lied and lied and lied. Now, you must tell the entire truth. You can always heal with the truth, no matter how ugly it is.

CLASSIC RESPONSE: My wife and I are on a good, positive roll, and I don't want to mess it up.

MY COMEBACK: Your positive roll won't last. Real healing is based on the truth.

CLASSIC RESPONSE: I'm worried she'll use the Document against me in court.

MY COMEBACK: Who are you, Perry Mason? Don't worry about court. Worry about saving your marriage. But thanks for the tip. I think your wife may want to use it in court. Is protecting yourself and your assets more important than saving your marriage and restoring your wife's faith in and love for you? [Wait for an answer; it will be very important.]

CLASSIC RESPONSE: I can't remember the details. I have a very poor memory.

MY COMEBACK: Nice try. You remembered her phone number, didn't you? You remembered to show up for dates you had with her, didn't you? Your memory is just fine. Your wife will always remember the pain that you inflicted on her. This is how to heal that pain.

CLASSIC RESPONSE: I'm a terrible writer. I haven't written a letter in years.

MY COMEBACK: We're not submitting this for publication. No one will check your grammar. Just do your best.

Feel free to use my responses to your husband's weak and insulting attempts to avoid writing the Document. If he reacts in any of these ways, it's obviously a very bad sign. Saving his marriage and winning back your love are not worth it to him. If you don't get an immediate apology and a sincere willingness to follow through with the Document, move right into shunning and separation mode.

HOW DOES HE CREATE THE DOCUMENT?

You can learn a great deal about your husband by observing how he carries out the Document assignment. The manner in which he completes the Document, the Document itself, and how he reads the Document to you—all reveal where his heart is. Is it with you and God *or* with this other woman—and Satan? Here's how a man with his heart in the right condition does the Document:

- He does it in a week or less.

- He takes it very seriously and works at it diligently every day.

- He does not throw it together at the last minute.

- It is at least two pages long.

- It is not general or vague, but detailed and specific.

- It is not a list, but a real letter with sentences and paragraphs.

- He expresses extreme sorrow for his adultery and says he's sorry many times.

- He begs for your forgiveness.

- He calls what he did sin, not a terrible mistake or a straying.

- It does not read like a love letter to his paramour.

- He does not protect or defend the adulteress or what they did in any way.

- He does not compliment his paramour in any way.

- He expresses no warm feelings for her now, just disgust and revulsion.

- He says that they "had sex," not that they "made love."

- He does not place on you one iota of blame for his adultery.

- He mentions confessing his sin to God and getting his spiritual life back on track.

- He does not read it in a stoic, angry, uncaring, or perfunctory way.
- He reads it with deep emotion, even tears and anguish.

If his Document shows he's not where he needs to be, you need to go into an even more aggressive, Matthew 18 stance. Pull back—pull way back—and hit him with the broadside of shunning and separation. When he breaks down and gets his attitude adjusted, he'll do the Document again. And this time, he'd better do it the right way.

A Sample Document

Read this Document. Although fairly brief and fictitious, it is an example of the correct way to do it.

Dear _____ [spouse's name]:

This is the hardest thing I have ever done. I'm so sorry, so very sorry for what I have done. I can't believe I did it, but I did. It was the worst choice of my life. My adultery with _____ [paramour's name] was completely and totally my fault. I have sinned against God, against you, and against the kids. I have betrayed you. I am ashamed.

I met _____ six months ago at work. It was in mid-January because she had just transferred in from Atlanta. I thought she was attractive, nice, and fun to be around. I had no romantic feelings for her at first. We were just friends—acquaintances, really. We'd talk and shoot the breeze on breaks and in the hallway. It went on this way until about mid-February. Then, something changed between us. It was the day after Valentine's Day, and she was upset. I asked her what was wrong, and she started to cry. She told me her husband had done nothing for Valentine's Day. By the way, she's thirty-five, been married about twelve years, and has two sons, one eight, and one ten.

Anyway, she poured out her heart to me about her bad marriage. Like a fool, I listened and tried to comfort her. I hugged her briefly after our twenty-minute talk.

Looking back, I see that's where I crossed the line. I began to feel differently about her. I asked her to lunch the next day. We both talked about our families, how we grew up, and about our spouses. I'm ashamed to say I told her the things I didn't like about you: your weight, your lack of time for me, and the way you kept the house. I told her I loved you, but I wasn't in love with you.

After that lunch, things really took off. We talked every chance we got at work. We went to lunch about three times a week. The first time I kissed her was in early April. We were in my car just after lunch, just sitting and talking. I asked her if I could kiss her, and she said yes. I reached over and kissed her. I pulled away, then we kissed again—a long and more passionate kiss.

We continued to talk at work and by cell phone and e-mail, as you now know. Most of our conversations were just about superficial things like how work was going, what we'd done the day before, plans for the weekend, and what our kids were up to. We did have a few deeper-type talks where we talked about our feelings for each other. I tried to help her improve her marriage, and she gave me advice on how to treat you better. How ridiculous! We were giving marital guidance in the middle of an affair!

She said she loved me one time—it was after a lunch, and we were alone in the elevator in our office building. I'm sorry to say that I said I loved her too. After that first kiss, we kissed and made out after every lunch in my car. We began to cut the lunch short so we could have more time to make out. We parked behind the Smith Bank most of the time. Two times we parked way back in the rear of the parking garage at work. My best guess is, we made out about thirty times. Approximately a half hour each time, always in my car. I fondled her genital areas many times and vice versa.

We had intercourse five times. Two times in the hotel on Elm Street: April 5 and April 15. I paid in cash, and we only stayed for a few hours each time. It was not safe sex. The other times were all at her place during the week in May when her husband and kids were out of town. The first two times, May 2 and 4, were during long lunch breaks. The last time, May 5, was that Friday I told you I had to work late. That was a lie like all the other lies. These were also not safe sex times. She told me she was on the pill, so we felt safe. I know how stupid that sounds now.

After May 5, we had one more lunch meeting, on May 8. We talked about our time at her house Friday and how much we enjoyed it. We agreed we shouldn't be together like this, but that was just talk. I wanted to be with her even though I knew it was wrong. Well, that was our last contact. You found those e-mail messages and cell phone records that afternoon and confronted me.

Honey, I want to say again how sorry I am for this sinful, disgusting relationship.

I don't love this woman. I never did. I just thought I did. I love you, and I always will. I promise you I will never have another affair. I promise you I will do anything to help you heal from what I've done. I beg you to forgive me. I will answer all your questions about my affair—anytime, anyplace. I want to rebuild our marriage, and with God's help, I know we can do it. I will change. I'll be a godly man. I'll be accountable to you and to a brother in Christ. I'll be a loving husband and a great dad. I know words are cheap, and you don't believe me. All I ask is for the chance to prove it to you.

Love,

NINE

IT'S TIME TO HEAL

*You Vent, You Question,
You Find Out Why*

The affair is over. He is not in contact with the other woman. He loves *you* and wants you back. He has read his Document to you. You know the terrible truth of what he has done—at least, most of it. Now comes the really hard part. For the next two to three months, you and your husband must directly face and talk through every facet of his adultery. You will leave no emotion unexpressed. You will leave no question unasked or unanswered. You will leave no reason or motivation unexplored.

The two of you will eat, sleep, and drink his adultery. Very likely, it will be the most excruciatingly painful experience you will ever endure. You'll wonder many times if this part of the recovery process will ever end. Believe me, if you do it the right way, it will end. And you will be healed from his sin and will be on your way to a new, healthy, and intimate marriage.

FROM LIES TO HEALING

In private places, always away from the children and everyone else, you and your husband will talk about his adultery. Over and over and over and over again. There is only one person who decides when these talks occur and how long each lasts. That's you, the victim of his adultery. If you want to talk about his sin, anytime and anyplace is the right time and place. You'll say, "I want to talk now," and he'll reply, "Of course, honey." You'll say, "It's 1:00 A.M., but I want to keep talking," and he'll say, "We'll keep going as long as you want to."

These talks will be every day for a while, often more than once a day. Obviously, you'll have to work around your jobs and the children's schedules. Occasionally, you (the victim) will decide to skip a day or cut short a talk about his unfaithfulness because you're exhausted, you're weary of it and want a break, or you're ill. Your husband is allowed to end one of these talks only when he's on the verge of losing his temper and saying or doing something stupid. At this point, he can call for a temporary halt. As soon as possible, he comes back to you and says, "I'm ready to go again. I'm sorry I got upset. I have no right to be upset about anything. Where were we?"

Your Emotions Must Be Vented

You will vent all your emotions with him. Your rage. Your fury. Your disgust. Your intense pain. Your feelings of betrayal. Your scorn. Your grief. Your sorrow. Your fears. Your insecurities. Your humiliation. Your broken heart. Your deep hurt and sadness. He will learn to *listen*, to *reflect back* your emotions. He'll be patient, kind, and gentle. He'll apologize in a heartfelt way again and again. He'll offer no explanations or excuses for his adultery. He'll take full, unqualified responsibility for what *he* did with this woman.

He'll learn how to feel your pain. He'll learn how to share personally with you. He'll learn how to emotionally connect with you. He'll cry in front of you as he sees what he has done to you. He'll do his best to comfort you. He'll stand in the violent gale force wind of your repeated rejection of him and come back for more.

Your Questions Must Be Asked

You'll ask him thousands of questions about his adulterous relationship, and he'll answer every one of them. And as with your venting of emotions, he'll be loving, kind, and gentle. He will surpass Job in the patience department. After he has listened to you and responded to all of your questions and helped you heal from his affair, you'll use him as the poster boy for patience. In your home it won't be "Wow! You've got the patience of Job" anymore. It'll be "Wow! You've got the patience of _____ [your husband's name]."

For a period of two to three months, you will obsess over the details of your husband's affair. Guess what? That's perfectly healthy and normal. You are obsessing *silently*, day and night, anyhow. In fact it's necessary to fully recover from the trauma he has brought into your life.

Many adulterers have complained to me, right in front of their wives, that "she's totally obsessed with my affair and is picking constantly at all the details!"

I always respond, "Of course, she's obsessing! You've had an affair! What do you expect her to do—ignore what happened? Just forget all about it? Don't you see that's impossible? Be glad she's obsessing and not divorcing you, you dummy!"

Your obsession is temporary and part of your recovery. To heal, you need the clearest possible picture of his adultery. Women, even more so than men, heal by carefully reconstructing the specific events in a trauma and then reacting to them emotionally. Once you know the basic sketch of his affair, go back over and over that period of time to flesh out the story. You'll go over your calendar to discover what was going on in your family's life during his affair. You'll need to know if he was with her at key family times:

"On my birthday, you got an early morning call. Was it her?"

"When you were late for Sue's dance recital, were you with her?"

"At the Christmas show, you were nervous and agitated and kept looking around. Was she in the audience?"

There are no silly questions. There are no stupid questions. There are no frivolous questions. No question is inappropriate. All your questions are valid and reasonable and purposeful. As you ask your questions and get his answers, everything will click into place. You'll realize, looking back, the reason for his strange behavior: the preoccupation, the absences, the lack of sexual desire, the irritability, the explanations that didn't seem to quite make sense. The more you find out, the more emotions you'll feel surging up inside. Spray them out with intensity and passion—all over him. Doing this will trigger a burst of venting, which is perfectly fine. You'll go back and forth between venting and asking questions, and often you'll do both at the same time.

You'll ask some of the questions repeatedly. Even after he has answered these questions many times, you'll still ask them. Again, there's nothing wrong with that. I tell couples in affair recovery: "She can ask the same question a million times, and you'd better answer it the same way a million times." You're looking for reassurance. If he humbly and kindly gives you the same answer every time, you receive a little more assurance. A little more security. A little more confidence.

PUMP THE WELL

Think of yourself as a well filled with nasty, decaying, hazardous waste. Your husband has dumped all this horrible stuff into your life. Now you've got to pump it out—again and again and again. You've got to keep the pump running all the time to make sure you get all the waste out. Venting your emotions and asking questions are the ways you pump it all out. The well is only so deep, but you don't know how deep. God knows, and He'll help you use this method of venting and questioning to clean it out totally. There are a certain number of questions you'll have to ask. There are a certain number of times you'll have to express your emotions. If you just keep at it, God will reveal to you that the well is finally dry and will begin to be pure again.

CREATE HEALING MOMENTS WITH THE MODE

I have a term for the conversations that you and your partner have about his affair. I call these repeated conversations *The Mode*. A huge part of my recovery program is getting couples into The Mode. You're in The Mode when the victim is running her pump— venting and asking questions—and the adulterer is handling her with patience, kindness, sensitivity, gentleness, and love.

Every time the two of you have an in-The-Mode interaction about his adultery, it is a *healing* moment. It might not seem to be because the positive impact is not felt immediately. After one of these conversations, you won't smile and hug your husband and say, "Hey, thanks for listening and answering all my questions. That was a real healing moment." Even if he has done a good job and handled himself well, you may still stomp off in a fury with reactivated pain. But underneath, a connection was made. A little bit of understanding, a little bit of respect, a little bit of trust was created. A little bit of healing took place. When you've had a certain number of these healing moments, the two of you and your marriage will be well on the way to recovering from his adultery.

When you get in The Mode and stay in The Mode, you will heal from the terrible blow he inflicted on you. All the pain is flushed out of your system, and you'll be able to forgive him. If he treats you with care and concern, you'll be able to give your heart back to him. You'll be able to love him again with complete confidence and passion. It's very common in the aftermath of adultery to lose your feelings of love for the one who committed adultery. The Mode can help you get those feelings back. And not just back the way they were before, but better and deeper.

WHEN THE ADULTERER RESISTS THE MODE

It's very common, but completely unacceptable, for the adulterer to fight your attempts to get into the healing mode. He doesn't want to hear your emotions. He doesn't want to answer your questions. He's huffy. He's impatient. He's defensive. He's angry. He's also an idiot if he acts in these ways. He's insulting you and creating even more pain for you!

If he acts in any of these outrageous ways, your response needs to be rapid and uncompromisingly tough. Here are some common complaints of the adulterer to avoid your venting and questioning behavior, and snappy responses for you to throw back at him:

ADULTERER'S COMPLAINT: Let it go. It's in the past. Let's move on.

YOUR RESPONSE: It's hard to move on when we're pulling the Queen Mary behind us. Your adultery will never be in the past until we deal with it directly. It will haunt us forever.

ADULTERER'S COMPLAINT: Please don't bring it up when I'm stressed from work or just before I go to bed.

YOUR RESPONSE: You're breaking my heart! I'd hate to have you lose sleep over something as trivial as your adultery. I'm not in the habit of scheduling the expression of my emotions. When I'm ready to talk, you'd better be ready to talk. Can you imagine how much sleep I lost when I learned of your relationship with this woman—and still lose?

ADULTERER'S COMPLAINT: Going over and over these details serves no purpose. It's just hurting us both.

YOUR RESPONSE: You're wrong once again. It serves many purposes. Read Dr. Clarke's book. [In fact, make that a requirement.] It does hurt, but it also heals.

ADULTERER'S COMPLAINT: You're talking way too much. You go on and on, and I can't take it.

YOUR RESPONSE: Be glad I'm talking to you. When I stop talking, you'd better be worried.

ADULTERER'S COMPLAINT: I get frustrated and angry when you come after me and pound me verbally.

YOUR RESPONSE: You get frustrated and angry? Get over it. You have no right to those feelings. I do.

ADULTERER'S COMPLAINT: You're too intense, too rude, too loud, too emotional!

YOUR RESPONSE: You ain't seen nothin' yet! Of course, I'm emotional. You had an affair! I'm supposed to be calm?

ADULTERER'S COMPLAINT: How long is this going to drag on? How many emotions and questions can one person have?

YOUR RESPONSE: It'll go on for as long as it takes to heal. Your affair dragged on for a long time, didn't it? And my hurt has dragged on. It's your fault I even have to do this!

ADULTERER'S COMPLAINT: Okay, that's it. I've had it. I'm through talking about it.

YOUR RESPONSE: Oh, no, you don't. You won't be the one to decide when enough is enough. I'll be the one who decides that. If you're through talking about your adultery, then we have nothing to talk about.

This last response is exactly what you need to say if his attitude remains poor and he won't get into The Mode with you. He is showing you that his commitment is absent, his love for you is weak (if it's there at all), and he has not been broken. If you don't see dramatic improvement in just a few days, stop talking to him completely. Go into shunning and separation. This will protect you from further damage and might get his attention.

THE DOCUMENT OF RESPONSE

To anchor you firmly in The Mode and accelerate your healing, you need to write your husband a letter expressing the impact that his adultery has had on you. I call this the Document of Response, and I ask the victim to begin writing it immediately after she has heard her husband's Document. She'll read it to her husband one week later in our next session. Again, if you're working without a therapist, read it to him at home when just the two of you are on the premises.

This letter tells him what he has done to you. It's a dumping ground for all the horrible pain he has inflicted on you with his adultery. Even though you verbalize your feelings before and after the Document of Response, the written expression of the pain opens up the floodgates inside you and begins a deep cleaning of your mind, body, and soul. It forces you to get fully in touch with your emotions. It forces you to face the specific events of his adultery and react to them. In the most graphic, personal way possible, your letter reveals to your husband the damage his adultery has caused you.

A SAMPLE DOCUMENT OF RESPONSE

_____ [no "Dear," just his name],

I'm writing words I never thought in my wildest, most hideous nightmare I'd ever write. I'm expressing feelings I never dreamed I'd _ever_ have need to express. I'm living a nightmare that I never expected in my wildest imagination to live. Because, you see, I love you and have loved you for __ years. And because, you see, you promised me this would never happen. In our marriage vows, you gave your word that you'd never, ever, be with another woman. I expected pain and tough times and misunderstandings in our marriage, and we've had our share. But adultery was the one thing I didn't have to worry about. Not my _____ [husband's name]!

And now, you've done it. You've destroyed our marriage vows—the most sacred and personal vows one human being can make to another. You've destroyed our marriage. I don't know if I'll ever be the same. My anger burns within me. Furious doesn't even approach how I feel. I'm in a rage at you for what you've done. How dare you treat me this way! You've betrayed me like no one else has ever betrayed me—or could ever betray me. I gave you my heart wholly and unconditionally. You've ground it to pieces under your boot.

I will never forget, until the day I die, that moment when I found your love note to _____ [the other woman's name]. I hate to even write her name—it makes me sick to see it on paper. When I saw the envelope, I thought, *How nice! My sweet husband has gotten me a card.* Then I opened it up and saw with horror and utter disbelief that it was written not to me but to *another woman*. My knees shook. My heart broke into a million pieces. I was devastated. I was humiliated. I was in such pain I thought I would die on the spot there in the hallway.

As we've discussed your affair over and over in the last few weeks, my emotions have been on a roller coaster. Rage, disgust, and deep hurt all coming in and out unpredictably. When I picture the two of you together in the places you went, it cuts me like a knife. You said loving things to *her!* Things that should have been said only to me! You shared special secrets with her that should have been only for me to hear. You even had sex with her. You touched her body in places you had—and should only have—touched me. You gave to her something precious that was not hers to have. It was mine! I am devastated. My heart is broken. My soul weeps for what it has lost—for what you threw away!

You are an unbelievably selfish, stupid, and sinful man. Instead of coming to me and telling me why you were unhappy in our marriage, you went to her. Well, I hope it was worth it. I hate you for what you've done to me. You've brought such agony into my life. I have to do all this work to heal because of you. I hate you because you've hurt my children as well. They see Mommy cry and be sad and not have the energy to be with them. They're scared and insecure, and it's your fault. Instead of modeling purity and faithfulness and love, their primary and most influential model in life has shown them the ultimate sin. Did you want them to go on to commit adultery, too, in their marriages?

This adultery is all your fault. Don't ever, ever, ever again blame me in the slightest way for your sin of adultery.

I could write five hundred pages, but frankly, you're not worth the time, the paper, and the ink. I honestly don't know if I can ever forgive you or trust you again. I don't know if I can ever love you the way I did before when I gave you all my love. With God's help and your hard work, maybe. That's the best I can do.

I offer you no guarantees. If you want our marriage to survive, you'd better work incredibly hard. You'd better be patient and kind and help me heal. You'd better listen to me all night long, night after night, if that's what it takes. You'd better love me tenderly even when I hate your guts. You'd better be accountable to at least one other man for the rest of your life.

You'd better stop being a workaholic and spend more time at home with us. Speaking of work, leave your job—now. That whore is there, and I won't tolerate that. You'd better trade your car in—now. She's been in that car. You'd better become the best husband in the world. I want communication. I want romance. I want my needs met.

I want *most of all* for you to become a spiritual man. A godly man. A man who is becoming sensitive to God and His leading, His Word, and His will. The spiritual leader in our marriage and home. If you don't do the things to make these things happen, then I don't want you. Just go away now if you're not man enough or you don't want to do them. I'm still in this marriage only because of my commitment to God. I'll stay, maybe, if you truly change in all these areas.

_____ [no "Love," just your name]

Observe carefully his reaction to your Document of Response. He ought to be completely broken. Any denial or rationalizations still left in him ought to be totally shredded by the time you've read the last word. If he responds favorably, you can afford to nurture a small hope. You may be on your way to true recovery. Stay wary, stay in The Mode, and keep working at the recovery process. Give him your letter so he can read it. If you continue to make progress as a couple, you'll burn both Documents—together—soon. It will be a symbol of your old marriage burning into ashes.

On the other hand, if he reacts poorly to your Document of Response, you'll know he's not where he needs to be. If he sits stoically and shows no emotion as you read it, he's not where he needs to be. If he gets angry and defensive, he's not where he needs to be. If your letter doesn't hit him like a ton of bricks, something's desperately wrong with him. He may be a goner. Pull back and do it quickly. Shun and separate as soon as possible.

From "I Don't Know" to "Here's Why I Did It"

> All the ways of a man are clean in his own sight,
> But the LORD weighs the motives. (Prov. 16:2)

God thinks motives are important. He judges us on why we act. If God looks at the motives behind sinful behavior, so should we.

"Honey, I'm so sorry for my affair. I don't know why I did it. Believe me, it'll never happen again." These words aren't very comforting, are they? They're just not good enough! You both need to find out why he *chose* to engage in an adulterous relationship.

He won't—in fact, he can't—change until he finds out why. "What factors put me in a position to sin against God, my wife, my children?" "How did I open the door to Satan?" "How did I ever think this relationship was okay?" He must answer these questions. If he doesn't know why it happened, he is likely to do it again. If he knows why, he can, with God's help, stop the behavior at its source.

You need to know why, or you'll never trust him again. Crossing your fingers and hoping that he doesn't commit adultery again and that he no longer has feelings for this woman is no way to live. It will hang like a pall over and continually inject doubt into your marriage. It likely will destroy the new relationship you try to establish. You'll have 100 percent confidence in him only when you know he has identified and fixed the reasons for his adultery.

When you're both in The Mode and you're pressing him for the details, he is forced to relive his crime and figure out how it happened. He'll find out how he was feeling and thinking at each stage of the adultery. He'll find out his motivations, rationalizations, needs, and weaknesses. Slowly and methodically, he'll go from "I don't know" to "Here's why I did it." From a spiritual standpoint, finding out how this happened could make all the difference.

Learning about where he was in his relationship with God, how the Lord and Christian disciplines fit into his lifestyle, could give him insight that will change him for a lifetime. And this could be the means by which he becomes the moral, godly man you want.

Together, you'll find out why. Then he can work with you (and your therapist) to address those areas in his life that led him to adultery. Where he was once weak and sinful, he will become strong and Spirit-led.

Here are the brief explanations of two affairs:

Story #1

He was the baby in his family and had always been selfish. His mother was cold and distant. His family taught him not to express his emotions. He played the strong, silent type and repressed his pain and frustrations. He refused to open up and talk personally with his wife, despite her repeated attempts to engage him. He had a deep, desperate need to connect with a woman, but would not risk being vulnerable with his wife. He knew Christ as his Savior, but his life was empty of spiritual vitality, of joy, of fellowship with the Lord. He tried to find intimacy by viewing of pornography regularly on the Internet and in videos. He was accountable to no one.

He met an attractive, younger coworker, and they began a friendship. He found it easy to talk to her and was flattered by her attention and warmth. Because he had not allowed his wife to meet his emotional needs, this woman began to meet them. For the first time in his life, he felt that he was close to another person (which is the natural result of being vulnerable and sharing personal feelings). The pseudointimacy he created with this woman was too strong to resist, and he succumbed to it.

Story #2

He was spoiled as a child and was never taught self-discipline and boundaries. He was irresponsible and immature as a child, as a teen, and now as an adult. He just never grew up. His natural charm and wit helped him gain some success in sales, but he hated his job and hated the responsibility of being a husband and father. He had trusted Christ for the forgiveness of his sins as a child, but had not grown in his faith. He knew Christ as Savior, but in no way gave over the control of his life to the Lord. He attended church but was not involved. To him, it was more of a social club.

His one great dream, which he nurtured for years in his mind, was to have enough money to quit his job and live a life of leisure. He wanted to sample the pleasures the world had to offer. Guess who Satan brought to him one day at a sales convention? A millionairess who had a house on the beach and liked to live in the fast lane. It was a perfect (and satanic), dysfunctional match. She offered him his sinful dream, and he took it, sex, mansion, and Porsche.

From Victim to Overcomer

I've watched many couples working their way through this phase of adultery recovery, so I am well aware that these two-and-a-half to three months of venting and questioning are extremely difficult. It runs exactly counter to your natural impulses. You will have many reasons not to get into The Mode. Despite what has happened, no matter how bad, you may still love him and long to have him back. You want to forgive him too quickly and easily. You hate confrontations. You're a passive, sweet person. You're not used to feeling and expressing deep anger and hurt. You're scared of driving him away. You want to stay in control for your kids, job, family, and friends. You want to avoid the terrible pain inside you.

It is imperative that you see these reasons for what they are: excuses that will keep you from healing. Some of the most seriously depressed, miserable women I've worked with are those who have repressed deep emotional pain caused them by their husbands' affairs. It's not pretty. They have continued to play the victim. Their husbands haven't changed; they merely said, "I'm sorry." And their marriages are awful. The incredible pain, the humiliation, the feelings of betrayal and their husbands' lack of love for them, their continual distrust of their husbands, all seethe beneath the surface. However, on the outside, they force a false image of happy, trustful, respected wives. Don't let this happen to you! I don't care if the affair ended years ago. You've still got to vent and question or nothing will change and everything will get worse.

There are two persons inside you. The first person loves her husband and wants to be kind, supportive, and compassionate. The second person is furious, deeply wounded—almost to the point of being terminal—and devastated. Be that second person *first*. It's safer and healthier for you, and you have the best chance to help your husband change and become the godly man you want him to become. As he shows real progress, you can let that first person out more and more. Is this conditional love? You bet it is! Offering conditional love is the way in which God wants us to deal with serious sinners. These are Jesus' words, recorded in Matthew 18:15–17:

> If your brother sins, go and reprove him in private; if he listens to you, you have won your brother. But if he does not listen to you, take one or two more with you, so that by the mouth of two or three witnesses every fact may be confirmed. And if he refuses to listen to them, tell it to the church; and if he refuses to listen even to the church, let him be to you as a Gentile and a tax-gatherer.

You can't get any more conditional than that. Follow these seven actions to get past your resistance and get into The Mode:

First, read Psalm 51—King David's words regarding his adultery—and list and number every feeling David had about his sin, its effect on him, and his every statement to God. Your husband should read this list and discuss with you the contents of this psalm and how he relates to it.

Second, reread the chapters in this book on anger (Chapters 5 and 6), and follow the exercises.

Third, tell your husband to ask you *every day* if you need to talk about his adultery.

Fourth, seek out a female accountability partner who will ask you *every day* if you've done your job of venting and questioning your husband. You will also vent emotions and pray with this trusted confidante.

Fifth, jot down on a pad emotions and questions that come up during the day. When you talk to your husband later in the day, you'll have these notes to help you.

Sixth, pour out your heart in a daily journal. Keep writing when the pain comes back. It's therapeutic. Plus, you can read it to your husband.

Seventh, pray out your pain again and again to the Lord, "casting all your anxiety upon Him, because He cares for you" (1 Peter 5:7). The Lord Jesus knows our suffering, even that of being betrayed by one He loved. God is the "God of all comfort" (2 Cor. 1:3).

I want you to keep a little-known fact in mind. For most couples, it's not the adultery itself that ends the marriage. It's the failure to work in a systematic, biblical way to heal from the adultery that ends the marriage. Do your work.

TEN

BACK AWAY
QUICKLY

*When to Shun
and How to Shun*

W hat do you do if . . .

- he refuses to end the affair?
- his attitude stinks?
- he's not broken and repentant?
- he refuses to make the final phone call?
- he has contact with his paramour again?
- he blames you in any way for his adultery?
- he refuses to leave a job where his paramour still works?
- he continues to have "feelings" for this person?
- he will not act immediately and get the AIDS and STD tests?
- he won't go to the counselor of *your* choice?
- he refuses to begin a spiritual growth/discipleship program?

- he won't be accountable to at least one godly man?
- he says he won't create the Document?
- he does not allow you to vent your emotions?
- he doesn't want to answer all your questions about his adultery?
- he doesn't work hard to find out why he committed adultery?
- he's not changing into a godly man, loving husband, and devoted father?

I'll tell you what to do if any of these things happen. You move into shunning and separation mode, and you do it as quickly as you can. It is the strongest and healthiest action you can take. It is biblical, as we've already seen in Matthew 18. It prevents what love you still have for him from draining away. It protects you and the kids. And it just might shake him up and turn him back to the Lord and to you.

To describe exactly what I mean by shunning and separation, I'll tell you the story of Mark and Sharon.

FIRST SESSION

In my first session with them as a couple, Mark admitted he had been having an affair for the past three months. Sharon had found out just five days earlier when she came across a love note from his paramour.

Mark began communicating with this woman on the Internet, moved to phone calls, and finally set up a meeting at a local restaurant. They talked nearly every day for three months. They met at parks, parking lots, restaurants, and motels. They had sex about fifteen times—all unprotected.

During the two-and-a-half months, before his adultery was discovered, Mark created a nasty smear campaign against Sharon. He told her he hadn't loved her for years because of her weight, her lack of affection for him, and her tendency to be negative and lose her temper. He used these issues to justify his coldness toward Sharon and his secret, ongoing affair. Sharon took his criticisms to heart because these areas were actual weaknesses in her life. She felt guilty, depressed, and totally responsible for Mark's rejection of her.

Mark wasn't satisfied merely with informing Sharon of her weaknesses. He told their pastor, close friends at church, and several neighbors the same story of how fat, unaffectionate, and angry Sharon had killed his love. He played the poor, suffering martyr role to the hilt and, unfortunately, got rave reviews. He fooled just about everyone. The pastor and most of their friends were counseling Sharon to lose weight, be affectionate, and control her temper in order to win Mark back.

In that first session I didn't like Mark's attitude, and I told him that. He acknowledged his adultery was wrong and all his fault, but he was angry and defensive. I asked him, "Do you really want to do the hard work to help Sharon heal from your adultery and to build a brand-new marriage?"

He replied with a sarcastic edge, "I'm here, aren't I?"

I told him showing up for a baseball game wasn't worth much if you didn't decide to play in it. After telling him he'd better get a new attitude in a hurry, I laid on him my recovery from adultery program. His mouth dropped open so wide I could see his tonsils. I told him that the next week would be the most important week of his now almost-destroyed marriage. I gave Sharon a license to blast him with her emotions and pump him with questions. I explained the Document carefully and informed Mark I wanted it completed for next week's session. Mark choked down his obvious surprise and anger and said he'd do all the steps.

SECOND SESSION

My concerns about Mark were confirmed in our second couple session. He made the final phone call, said he had no feelings for his partner in adultery, took his AIDS and STD tests, set up a meeting with their pastor to tell him everything and ask for a discipleship program, and completed the Document. But his attitude had not improved. Sharon told me he was listening to her vent and answering her questions, but only with great effort.

Mark read his Document, and I wasn't surprised to find it brief, superficial, and vague. I told him the letter was hardly the heartfelt, specific confession of a broken man who loved his wife. I told him to do the Document again and, this time, do it right. I told him he was digging his hole deeper and losing his opportunity to win his wife back. I again stressed the need for him to get into The Mode with Sharon.

I asked him to leave my office because I wanted a few minutes alone with Sharon. I told her Mark's attitude was awful and she needed to get angry at him. I said if his attitude didn't dramatically improve in twenty-four hours, call me and we'd go to Plan B.

IT'S TIME TO SHUN

Twenty-four hours later, Sharon called me and came in for an individual session. She told me Mark's attitude and treatment of her had not improved. In fact, he was running his smear campaign again. He was blaming her for their marital problems and for his affair. He'd stated he didn't know how he felt about Sharon anymore. He was refusing to let her vent and wouldn't answer any more questions about his adultery. He tried to convince her that I was a terrible psychologist who was causing more damage to their relationship. He told her to "get over it and stop digging up the past."

Sharon asked me: "What's Plan B?"

What I told her, I'm going to tell you:

Plan B is to shun him. The Bible teaches us to follow a progressive series of steps when dealing with someone who chooses to continue in serious sin. First, you warn the person (1 Thess. 5:14; Titus 3:10–11). Second, you shun the person (1 Cor. 5: 9–11; 2 Thess. 3:6, 14–15). Third, you separate from the person (Matt. 18:15–17).

Go home and give your husband two warnings. You can give both warnings today or one today and one tomorrow. Don't take more than two days to deliver these two warnings. Time is critical. He has slipped back into serious sin, and we have to act quickly to jar him back to repentance and reality. The longer his sin is allowed to go on without a response from you, the deeper it will get. You can communicate these warnings over the phone, in person, or in a note.

Tell him you're angry and very disappointed by his disgraceful, damaging, and sinful treatment of you. His adultery was, by itself, a terrible blow to you. Now, his rotten attitude and refusal to abide by Dr. Clarke's recovery program is rubbing salt into your wound. Inform him that you will not tolerate his sin any longer. Make it clear that if he doesn't give you a heartfelt apology and get back on the recovery track, he'll face serious consequences. Don't tell him what the consequences will be. Let him wonder.

Send this message and don't wait for a response. If you use the phone, hang up without saying good-bye. If you do it in person, say your piece and abruptly walk away. If you write him, don't bring up the letter later or ask for a response.

After your two warnings in a two-day period, move immediately into shunning mode if he hasn't responded with brokenness and repentance. Don't explain to him what you're doing. Just start shunning him.

As the shunning begins, call a private meeting with your children who live in the home. (You'll telephone and talk with those who no longer live in the house full-time.) Your husband is not invited to or welcome at this meeting. Give your children this message:

> Your father and I are having problems in our marriage. These problems have nothing to do with you but are due to things your father is doing. It is very serious. Your father is sinning [depending on the ages of the children, you might say, Your father is doing things that are wrong—bad]. He's treating me terribly, and I won't tolerate it any longer. So I'm not talking to him or doing things for him until he confesses his sin and begins to treat me in the way the Bible teaches a husband to treat his wife.
>
> We are being helped by a person who helps marriages. He has asked us to do certain things to help repair our marriage. Your dad has refused to do these things. If you want to know specifically how your father is sinning, ask him. If he continues his sin and mistreatment of me, I'll be forced to take some more steps. If that happens, I'll call another meeting and tell you exactly what I'll be doing and why.
>
> Now, let's pray for Dad to be broken before the Lord and to start acting like a godly man.

Your children need to know why you suddenly will be ignoring their father. If you don't give them at least a general explanation, they'll be confused and could potentially blame you for being so hard on Dad. Don't tell them about the affair—yet. If the shunning works, and your husband gets back on the recovery track, we can shield them from the trauma of finding out about his affair. As you shun him, if he tries to turn the children against you, then you have no choice but to sit down and tell them about their father's adultery. No gory details. Just the horrible fact that he has had an adulterous relationship with another woman and he is not working to help you heal. If they are preteens or younger, you will explain it using words they will understand.

I'm not going to beat around the bush. Just being told of the marital problems and then watching you shun their father will stress your kids to the max. Your honesty with them will help reduce their level of insecurity and pain. Realizing Mom and Dad are very unhappy, and not being told anything about it, is terrifying to children. Usually, the picture that children create is far worse than the actual situation. But the whole ongoing situation is still very traumatic for them.

Knowing what's going on provides the best protection you can give your children. Knowing what's going on helps them begin their adjustment to a possible separation and/or divorce. We don't want a separation or a divorce; that is the reason for this painful recovery program. But if your husband continues on his sinful path, it could happen. It's better for your kids to start dealing with this possibility now than to cruise ignorantly along and suddenly be told your marriage is in terrible shape and you have to separate. This trauma is far worse than the trauma created by telling them up front what's going on.

Plus, the pained reaction of your children to your shuns may help break your husband. As he sees their shock and anguish, maybe he'll realize what he's doing. As he attempts to answer their questions about what's going on, maybe he'll realize what he's doing. What he's putting your kids through now is merely a short preview of what they'll endure if a divorce occurs. Maybe that truth will dawn on him. Even if it doesn't, you and the kids will be well on your way to adjusting to life without him in the home.

Seriously consider going with your children to a Christian family therapist. If the therapist you are presently seeing has experience working with children, you could continue with him or her. Your kids need to express their pain, deal openly with the trauma and tremendous loss Dad is causing, and begin adjusting to the possibility of life without him in the home.

"You Don't Exist"

After you talk with the kids, take your wedding ring off, and shun your husband for the next five full days. If he breaks and says he's sorry one thousand times and begs to get back to the recovery program, you can stop shunning. But if he refuses to come around, go the full five days.

Shunning means you go as far as you can in an attempt to act as though he doesn't exist. You bring communication down to the lowest level possible. Unless you absolutely have to—money issues, the children's schedule, health emergencies—say nothing to him. Nothing at all. No "hello." No "good morning." No "how was your day?" When he talks to you, ignore him. When he asks you questions, don't answer them.

Like an idiot, he'll probably ask you, "Why are you doing this?" Say nothing. He knows exactly why you're doing it. He'd love to get you into an argument. But the time for arguing and fighting with him is over. He wants to know he can still get a rise out of you because that will mean he still has room to maneuver and manipulate. You want him to believe that you're over him. That you don't care anymore. That you are not in the slightest bit interested in the man he has chosen to become. That nothing he can do, except repent, means a thing to you. When you must say something to him, be as brief and businesslike and cold as you can possibly be.

I want you to stop all services for your husband. No sex. Period. In fact, allow no physical affection of any kind. He has lost, for at least five days, the sacred privilege of coming near you physically. Don't sleep in the same bed with him during the shunning period. Without a word move his pillow and a sheet and blankets to a guest room or the living room couch. If there's another bathroom in the house he can use, move all of his toiletries in there. If you have another room he can live in, move all of his clothes in there.

If he moves all of his stuff back into your bedroom and bathroom and refuses to move out, then you move to the other bedroom and bathroom. It ought to give you the creeps to be in the same bed with him, to be in the same bedroom with him, and to share the same bathroom with him. So don't do it.

Don't do any laundry for him. Don't iron any clothes for him. Don't buy anything for him. Don't run any errands for him. Don't set a place for him at the table. Don't prepare any food for him. Make meals for you and the children. He's on his own and can forage for himself at mealtimes. If he sits down at the table and takes food, let him eat. Just ignore him.

During these five days of shunning, avoid all social contact with him. No dates. No talks of any kind. Don't sit with him at church or at any school functions if these meetings fall in the five-day period. Don't drive in the car with him. Don't spend any family time with him and the kids. You're not a happy family thanks to him, so don't pretend.

What you're doing with the shunning is turning the tables on him. Until now, the script read "Oh, no! I'm losing him!" Now, it reads "Oh, no! He's losing me!" You're giving him a taste of life without you, which he has set up by his betrayal of you. You're giving him—actually, cramming it down his throat—a taste of divorce. Will he like it? You'll find out over the next five days.

Your husband's reaction to your shuns will reveal his true character, his spiritual condition, his commitment to you, and his love for you. Many women have asked me two questions when I explain shunning. Here they are, with my answers:

QUESTION: Won't this shunning drive my husband farther away from me?

ANSWER: Yes, it sure might. If it does, there's your answer. He doesn't love God and doesn't want to come back to Him. He doesn't love you. And he's not willing to change.

QUESTION: Will shunning make him run back to the other woman?

ANSWER: Yes, it sure might. If he returns to her, he has made his choice. He found her more attractive than you, was willing to hurt you beyond belief and to destroy your home. Now he is confirming what his actions indicated. If you require nothing of him but an apology and a promise not to do this again, you have held on to this kind of man. There's your answer.

Sharon left my office determined to shun Mark. I scheduled our next session for seven days hence. I told her to bring Mark to that session only if his firewall of denial, arrogance, and wickedness had been broken.

ELEVEN

BRING DOWN THE HAMMER

*When All Else Fails,
Separate*

Sharon came alone to the third session. She told me Mark seemed to soften on the second day of shunning. But when she didn't immediately forgive him and agree to have sex with him, he blasted her verbally and went right back to his angry, mean, sinful self. Sharon said to me: "Well, I guess we're at the Matthew 18 step, aren't we?"

MATTHEW 18 AND SEPARATION

I replied, "Yes, that's exactly where we are. Matthew 18:15–17 is the third and final step in dealing with a person who refuses to stop sinning. This chilling, sledgehammer-to-the-head passage ends with the sinner being removed from the local body of Christ. I believe there is clear application to the marriage relationship. There are no qualifiers in this passage. No exceptions are made for spouses. You, his spouse, are in the local body of Christ. So you, too, are to remove him from your presence. That means from your home."

Here's the advice I gave Sharon:

GET PREPARED FINANCIALLY

First, I want you to get prepared for separation in the financial area. It will be your husband's responsibility to pay for your expenses and the children's expenses during separation, but he can't be trusted. Many husbands try to squeeze their wives with money when they're kicked out of the home. Continue shunning, and spend the next week getting your financial house in order. As quietly and secretly as you can, get copies of all financial records (bank accounts, investment accounts, savings accounts, retirement accounts, his 401K, his business records if he owns his own business, insurance policies, credit card information), and keep them in a safe place outside your home. Call your CPA, insurance agent, and investment advisor, and have these professionals send you copies of everything.

See a reputable and tough attorney and find out what you can do in your state, short of divorce, to protect you and your kids financially during a separation. If you are able to file for a legal separation or a separate maintenance agreement under which your husband is forced to provide for your needs, get the paperwork started. If you can legally attach your name to major assets that do not now carry your name (home, cars, property, investment accounts), start that process. When you do separate, you'll have to be ready to move fast in these legal areas.

Start your own checking and savings accounts now. Be ready, with your attorney's advice and guidance, to transfer half of the joint account money into these separate, your-name-only accounts. Your husband will be outraged and say, "You don't trust me!" To which you'll reply with the world's biggest "Duh!"

Ask family, close friends, church members, and church leaders to be ready to help you with money if separation occurs. Ask these same persons for help with the kids and in other practical areas.

THE FINAL STEPS

With your finances in order, you can move quickly through the Matthew 18 steps. You've already confronted him one-on-one, so it's time to confront him with one or two witnesses. This instruction to use witnesses is originally taught in Deuteronomy 19:15 and is given in John 8:17; 2 Corinthians 13:1; and 1 Timothy 5:19. Go to your husband with one or two family members, close friends, and/or church leaders. Include at least one man. Prior to the meeting with him, tell these witnesses everything that has happened up to that point. Let them do the talking during the intervention.

If he does not immediately—and I mean immediately—respond with brokenness, go with the witnesses to the leaders of your church. Ask the leaders to follow Matthew 18 and confront him quickly, and remove him from the church body if he chooses not to repent.

If your church leaders move with haste and excommunicate him in a matter of two weeks or less, you can wait until he's out of the church to separate from him. The reality is, most church boards move slowly, if at all, in the church discipline of confrontation. If they're dragging their feet, you don't have time to wait. Often an adulterer will flatly refuse to meet with anyone, so this response also necessitates immediate action. Your marriage—not to mention the emotional and spiritual health of you and your children—hangs in the balance. Go ahead and separate immediately.

Separation is the absolute last resort. And that's where we are. It will keep you and the kids from being destroyed. It will keep whatever love that still exists between you and your husband from being crushed. If you continue to live with a man who abuses you, all your love will be gone eventually. Separation may turn him back to God and restore him as your godly husband and father of your children. Let's hope you can experience what Matthew 18:15 talks about: "If he listens to you, you have won your brother."

TELL YOUR CHILDREN THE TRUTH

Assuming he does not respond, and you must separate, the next step is to talk to your children. Just as you did prior to shunning, gather your children and tell them what's going to happen and why. In terms the younger children will understand, tell them their father has continued to sin and now you will attempt to separate from him. Read Matthew 18:15–17 out loud and explain your reasoning. If you haven't already, tell them their father has had an affair. Don't go into detail, but make it clear that Dad has had an adulterous relationship with another woman and that's what all these problems are about. His adultery and continued refusal to "be sorry" and do what is right are the reasons that you are telling him to leave the home.

If you don't tell the children about his adultery, they have no explanation about why Mom is being so upset with Dad and is taking the dramatic step of separation. They need to know exactly why you're being so hard on Dad, or they'll blame you for what's happening and may side with their sinning father. Or they'll blame themselves.

You are enabling your husband and actually aiding him to escape the full impact and consequences of his sin. Keeping his adultery a secret will make it easy for him to convince the children that the separation and marital problems are your fault too. The truth is, it's all his fault!

You're lying to your children. When they discover your lie, they'll be devastated and feel betrayed by you. They'll wonder what else Mom has told them that isn't true. The one person they looked to for truth and integrity can't be trusted anymore.

You lose a powerful opportunity to force your husband to face the destructive results of his adultery. The pain that the truth brings to his children may cause him to finally come to his senses.

I recommend telling all your children ages five and up. For younger children, put it in terms they can at least partly grasp: "Daddy has done bad things with another woman. He liked another woman in a way he's only supposed to like me. Mommy is angry and sad because he did this and because he won't help me feel better."

After Dad leaves the home, have regular family meetings where all members are encouraged to vent their emotions about what Dad has done and about the separation. Pray for God's strength and comfort at these meetings and, of course, for Daddy. It's okay—in fact, important—for you to express your pain and anger in front of the children, but not in a way that implies a lack of control or faith. That will keep you strong and will model sharing emotions for them. Keep assuring them that you're going to make it. Go with them to a Christian family therapist. With God's help you and the kids will make it.

Move Him Out

The time has come to get rid of him. Don't ask him to leave. Don't wait for him to decide to leave. Move him out in a sudden, surprise attack that will hit him like a tidal wave. Invite several friends (at least one should be a man) over to your house, and when your husband is at work, bag up all his personal possessions: clothes, tools, knickknacks, toiletries, golf clubs and other sporting equipment, laptop computer, whatever. With the exception of furniture, include every item he'd get in a divorce. Throw in your wedding album too. Use garbage bags because that sends the appropriate message.

Change the locks on all the doors, and then with your support team around you, call him with the news: "You've decided not to repent of your sin after repeated confrontations. That's your choice. You are no longer welcome in my home. Some friends and I have packed up all your stuff, and it's on the driveway. Come and pick it up when you want. You'd better hurry; it looks like rain."

One of my clients got a little creative in the moving-him-out process. She put the microwave on the driveway with an exploded lasagna casserole all over the inside. She put this note inside: "To be picked up by my lying, adulterous, soon-to-be ex-husband."

Make sure your support team stays with you until he comes to the home. Don't let him in the house. Legally, you cannot remove him from the house or apartment. Morally, you can, and you should. If he shows up with the police, you'll have to let him in the house. Some men are so evil and stiff-necked that they will refuse to leave the home. In that case, at least you've made your point. You'll have to continue the shunning indefinitely. Not many men can stand to be shunned for long, so he might leave after a few weeks.

If he's in a rage and you fear he may be dangerous, take the children and leave immediately. With a police escort and your friends to accompany you, you can go back to gather what you and the children will need in order to live outside the home.

If he threatens you or physically handles you in any way, call the police and file for a restraining order.

MAKE IT A REAL SEPARATION

When he is out (and most men will leave when booted out this way), the separation needs to be a complete separation. It needs to be a "hell has no fury like a woman scorned" separation. Have no contact with him except to cope with emergencies, to discuss money, and to deal with the children. No friendly chitchats, in person or on the phone. These little fireside chats ease his guilty conscience and remove all the impact of the separation. You don't want to make him comfortable. You want to make him miserable.

You have nothing to say to him. You are as cold and unmoving as a glacier. The only talking you'll do is to his friends and his family. Of course, you'll inform both families and your friends about his sin and the separation. Tell all those persons about the affair and his refusal to rebuild the marriage. If they want to try to talk some sense into him, fine.

He'll want to come in the house when he just "drops by" or is picking up the kids. Don't let him in. Set up a strict visitation schedule he will follow to see the children. Use the exact schedule that a court would order in a divorce. Ask an attorney what this schedule would be. When he comes to get the kids, let him honk the horn or stand on the porch. You'll send the kids out to him and shut the door behind them. When he drops them off, say nothing, and don't look at him. Just shuffle the kids back inside.

Just as when you were shunning him, include him in no family times. Don't sit with him in church or at school functions and sports events. Don't invite him to the kids' birthday celebrations. He can set up his own birthday parties for them. Don't get together with him for Easter, Thanksgiving, Christmas, New Year's Day, Groundhog Day, or any other holiday.

And please—please—don't go on any vacations with him or invite him when you and the children go on vacation! I don't know how many clients have whined to me: "Oh, but Dr. Clarke, this vacation has been scheduled for months!" My response is: "His affair was scheduled for months too!" Would you go on a vacation with a man you'd just discovered was Jack the Ripper if it had been planned for months? Don't be a pathetic wimp. Stay home or go on your own vacation.

Don't ask for his help for anything. Don't let him mow your lawn. Don't let him clean the pool. Don't let him fix the appliances or do any home repairs. Don't let him take care of your car. If you allow any of these things, that's not a separation. That's not what happens after a divorce. You don't want him to feel like a good, magnanimous, helping guy. You want him to feel like a pariah. A wretched, lost soul who's on the outside—of your and your children's love and respect—looking in. Ask family, friends, neighbors, and church members to help you repair things, or hire repair persons.

This complete separation sends your husband the best message you can send him: "I will not tolerate your mistreatment any longer. You are considering life apart from me, so here's what it's like. You've lost me. It's over." You're giving him a full taste of divorce. Make him believe you are through with him and your marriage, and you're moving on to better things.

If your husband doesn't come around and get back on the recovery track, you have your answer. He doesn't want you or the marriage, and he'll continue to be involved in serious, ongoing sin. I never recommend divorce. Stay separated and pray for God's guidance. God will reveal what He wants you to do. The separation will give you a good head start in adjusting to life without your husband.

When to End the Separation

If he makes any noises about being sorry and wanting to get back together, don't believe him. Don't get your hopes up and let him back in the home. That's a classic mistake and one of the most common mistakes victimized spouses make in this separation process. It will lead to disaster. Schedule a phone call with him. In this conversation tell him that words are cheap, and he'll have to work very hard for a very long time to have any chance of living with you again. With no guarantee at all that there will be a reconciliation, he'd better get back into the recovery mode and make all the changes you ask him to make.

In a letter or in this same telephone conversation, inform him of certain steps he must take if he's serious about wanting to bring his marriage back from the dead. If you do it by phone, advise him to take careful notes because he'd better not miss even one point. Here's the list you lay on him:

1. The complete separation will last at least the next two months. During this time, you will have no contact with him other than what is absolutely necessary.

2. He will regularly see the counselor of *your* choice (a minimum of once a week), and meet with the spiritual mentor of your choice (one of your pastors or another mature, godly man) weekly during the next two months. He will sign releases so both these men can give you updates on his progress, how they perceive his attitude, his spiritual health, and so on.

3. He'll work with the previously mentioned Christian counselor (a licensed, master's degree therapist or a Ph.D. psychologist) to find out why he had the affair, why he treated you so badly, and why he initially refused to work the recovery program. He'll take a penetrating look at his family, unresolved pain and traumas in the past, and his weaknesses as a person, husband, and father. Over a two month period, he will see the counselor at least eight times.

4. With the guidance of the counselor, he'll write you a series of honest, open, and intensely personal letters explaining in detail what he's discovered about the areas mentioned in Point 3.

5. He will write you the complete truth about his adultery, including any additional contact of any kind he has had with the paramour since he told you he stopped the relationship.

6. Under the supervision of his spiritual mentor, he will embark on a path of spiritual discovery and growth. He'll read and study the Bible. He'll memorize Proverbs 5 and recite it to you over the phone with his mentor by his side. He'll be in a men's small group and a discipleship/accountability program. He will attend church services every time one is held. As stated earlier, he'll be accountable to one godly man at least once a week. He will return to his first love, Jesus Christ.

7. He will sign a legal, witnessed, and notarized document that states that if he ever has another affair, he will give you the home, the life insurance, big-time alimony (ask your attorney for a figure), and custody of the children.

8. He will, in the presence of his counselor or spiritual mentor, call all the family members and friends to whom he has lied and who he has hurt with his sin and offer a heartfelt apology.

If he does all these things during the two months of total separation, and his counselor and his spiritual mentor tell you they think he's genuinely changing, then you can agree to reenter marriage therapy and continue the recovery from adultery work. If these steps take him longer than two months, you will wait until he's where he needs to be. Keep in mind, even after you're back in marriage therapy, you remain separated until you know this man has turned the corner. You need to make absolutely sure he has changed before you let him back in the house. I repeat: it is vital that you do not—out of loneliness, need, your desperate desire to restore the marriage, or for any other reason—violate this rule. If you allow him back and you attempt a new marriage too soon, the next breach will probably be the end of the marriage.

If he goes back to his old ways, you'll end marriage therapy and continue the complete separation. He'll have to go back to work on himself, and it will take even longer this time to prove to you he's ready for couple counseling.

The Rest of the Story

Mark and Sharon's separation lasted a full five months. At the month-and-a-half mark, Mark finally broke and decided to change. He worked hard to follow my eight-point program for a separated, adulterous spouse. I saw him for eight sessions, and he uncovered a lot of pain in his past. I had him write tough, honest, and loving letters to both his parents. And I had him send them. He also sent a series of letters to Sharon. He grew emotionally and, more important, spiritually.

After two months of working with me and with his pastor, he was ready for marriage therapy again. Sharon came in, and we did a month and a half of couple work before they resumed living together as man and wife. I saw them four times after they moved in together.

They were happy. They were healed. They were in a completely different marriage. They were one in Christ. Mark had confessed, repented, and knew forgiveness of a great sin. Like the woman taken in adultery—"in the very act"—who was brought to the Lord Jesus, Sharon's husband, Mark, heeded Jesus' words: "Neither do I condemn you; go your way. From now on sin no more" (John 8:11). And like "the woman who was a sinner" who wept at Jesus' feet and anointed them with costly ointment, Mark learned the truth of Jesus' words to her: "Her sins, which are many, have been forgiven, for she loved much; but he who is forgiven little, loves little" (Luke 7:47).

Mark and Sharon built a brand-new marriage *only* because Sharon followed a tough, no-nonsense, biblical approach to Mark's sin. Sharon believed that my approach was what God wanted her to do. I want you to believe it is too.

If you do anything short of the shunning and separation I've described in these last two chapters, you are enabling your spouse. If you put up with sinful behavior, he'll keep slamming you with it. You will actually encourage and become a part of his sin. You'll be partly responsible for the increased, ongoing damage done to you, your kids, and your marriage. Don't do that!

Shunning and separation are your final attempts to rock his mixed-up, Satan-controlled world and bring him to his knees before God. What you must see and feel in your alienated spouse is the "broken and contrite heart" of Psalm 51:17. Without that, you have nothing, and your marriage is over. With it anything is possible.

TWELVE

THE BIBLE'S APPROACH
IS THE BEST APPROACH

What God Says About
Marriage and Adultery

I've already provided scriptural support for my program, but I think it's important to go one step further. I want you to see, in one chapter, that the entire picture of what I am recommending is rooted in the teachings of the Bible.

Marriage is a sacred institution established by God. The "one flesh" relationship described in Genesis 2:24 is to be the deepest intimacy possible between a man and a woman: "For this cause a man shall leave his father and his mother, and shall cleave to his wife; and they shall become one flesh." Two previously separate individuals become one with each other and with God.

Marriage is a physical, emotional, and spiritual covenant that God expects to be permanent. Read the words of Jesus: "Consequently they are no longer two, but one flesh. What therefore God has joined together, let no man separate" (Matt. 19:6).

God Himself joins a man and a woman in marriage. It isn't merely some legal arrangement or relationship of convenience. It is a bond created and sealed by the God of the universe. Jesus said, "Let no man separate." Those powerful words pack a serious warning.

The prophet Malachi, using brutal and harsh words, condemned Israelite men who were divorcing their wives for no good reason. He told the men that God was rejecting their offerings: "Because the LORD has been a witness between you and the wife of your youth, against whom you have dealt treacherously, though she is your companion and your wife by covenant" (Mal. 2:14).

Just in case the "treacherous" men didn't fully grasp God's view of divorce, Malachi drove it home with a vengeance: "'For I hate divorce,' says the LORD, the God of Israel, 'and him who covers his garment with wrong,' says the LORD of hosts. 'So take heed to your spirit, that you do not deal treacherously'" (Mal. 2:16).

Read the first sentence of Malachi 2:16 again carefully. The first part—God hates divorce—is clear. The second part—God hates "him who covers his garment with wrong"—is often overlooked. Referring to the man who divorces his wife—"his faithless treatment of the wife in putting her away"—Old Testament scholars Keil and Delitzsch give their view:

> A second reason for condemning the divorce is . . . "he (who puts away his wife) covers his garment with sin," or "sin covers his garment." The meaning is the same in either case, namely, that wickedness will adhere irremovably to such a man . . . the dress reflects the inward part of a man, and therefore a soiled garment is a symbol of uncleanness of heart. (C. F. Keil and F. Delitzsch, *Biblical Commentary on the Old Testament*, vol. 2, *Minor Prophets* [Grand Rapids: Eerdmans, 1967], 452–54)

In *A Commentary Critical, Experimental and Practical on the Old and New Testaments*, A. R. Fausset writes this about the husband who faithlessly commits the act that the Lord God hates:

THE BIBLE'S APPROACH IS THE BEST APPROACH

"Whereas they ought to have spread the skirt of their garment over their wives, for the protection of those so dear, they covered their garment with violence toward them" (Robert Jamieson, A. R. Fausset, and David Brown [Grand Rapids: Eerdmans, 1967], 4:719). Marriage is so important to God that if you break it for unacceptable reasons, He hates you. This may sound harsh and uncharacteristic of God, but that is how holy the institution of marriage is to Him. I do realize that Christ died for this sin, too, and if you truly confess and *repent* (that is, turn from destroying your marriage to restoring it), He will forgive you in love.

In Ephesians 5:25 Paul had this to say about marriage: "Husbands, love your wives, just as Christ also loved the church and gave Himself up for her." Marriage pictures the relationship that Jesus has with us, His children! You don't get any more sacred and meaningful than that.

God created marriage. The marriage relationship is precious to Him. It is the bedrock of the family. It is the most important human relationship. It is a wonderful gift to us. It is a beautiful picture of Christ's unconditional love and care for His church. You'd better not fool with it.

ADULTERY BREAKS THE MARRIAGE BOND

An affair is one of the most vicious attacks possible on a marriage. The only thing worse would be your husband trying to kill you physically. He has certainly killed your marriage and just about killed you emotionally by being with another woman. Adultery strikes at the very heart of a marriage because it destroys the oneness God has created. Sexual purity is an essential part of a healthy marriage: "Let marriage be held in honor among all, and let the marriage bed be undefiled; for fornicators and adulterers God will judge" (Heb. 13:4).

Your husband has dishonored your marriage. He has defiled your marriage bed. He has shattered your marriage vows and ground them under his heel. With his adultery he has broken the seventh commandment of God. He has broken the first commandment because his mistress is an idol. He has broken the fifth commandment because he has dishonored his parents. He has broken the ninth commandment because of all the lying he has done. He has also broken the tenth commandment by coveting someone who is not his.

Your adulterous husband has sinned against you, your family, your extended family, the church, and God. He has committed serious sin. Martin Luther's disgust and hatred of adultery led him to write that with the exception of idolatry and unbelief, God punishes no sin as severely as He does sexual misconduct. He wrote that adultery is worse than any theft, for no restitution can be made to the injured spouse.

And according to the Bible, serious sin requires—indeed, demands—a serious response.

GOD SAYS, "CONFRONT SIN"

What does the Bible teach us to do about sin? Confront it and the sinner. Every single time. God confronted sin in the Israelites again and again. Jesus Christ confronted sin in the Pharisees (Matt. 23:13–36) and in His disciples (Matt. 16:23; Mark 9:33–37). In his letters to New Testament churches, Paul confronted their sins without hesitation. It was vital to maintaining their spiritual health and vitality and testimony. On the personal level, when Peter was sinning, Paul "opposed him to his face" (Gal. 2:11).

The Bible's teaching on confronting people in sin is not popular in American churches. It swims against the current in many churches in our culture. It is not a good public relations message; it is not the way to fill pews. Confronting sinners is awkward,

THE BIBLE'S APPROACH IS THE BEST APPROACH

difficult, and painful. You won't hear many sermons on Matthew 18 and other confrontation passages. You won't see much confronting going on in churches. Looking the other way is a whole lot easier. It's also the opposite of what the Bible tells us to do.

If there is an unresolved issue between you and another person, you are to go *immediately* to that person and try to make it right (Matt. 5:23–24). You are to speak "the truth in love" (Eph. 4:15). Like Paul in 1 Corinthians 10, be bold in confronting sinners. Be as tough as Paul was when he confronted sinners in Corinth: "I already gave you a warning when I was with you the second time. I now repeat it while absent: On my return I will not spare those who sinned earlier or any of the others" (2 Cor. 13:2 NIV).

You cannot control how the sinner responds to the confrontation. That is his responsibility, and God will hold him accountable for his actions. Your responsibility before God is to confront him.

When King David committed adultery with another man's wife and, to cover up his sin, had sent the woman's husband to the front lines of a war to be killed, God's prophet told him, "You are the man!" (2 Sam. 12:7). God's punishment of David was severe and affected all of Israel.

If you refuse to confront sin, you are violating the clear teaching of Scripture. If you refuse to confront the sin of your husband, you enable it. You support it. You approve it. You actually encourage it. And that causes you to sin because you're not doing what the Bible tells you to do.

How to Confront

When a person chooses not to stop some form of serious sin, the correct response is to shun him. Ignore him. Cut him off. Act as if he doesn't exist. Is this brutal? Yeah, it sure is. Is it biblical? You bet it is.

In 2 Thessalonians 3:14–15, Paul advised Christians to socially ostracize a fellow believer who was lazy and would not work. Paul wanted the unproductive sinner to feel shame and so be motivated to get back to work. He wrote to Titus giving these specific instructions on dealing with someone who was threatening the unity of the church: "Warn a divisive person once, and then warn him a second time. After that, have nothing to do with him. You may be sure that such a man is warped and sinful; he is self-condemned" (Titus 3:10–11 NIV).

Two strikes and you're out. When a person will not repent after two warnings, your job is to completely pull back from him. The same principle applies to an adulterous husband. As I've indicated, first you'll shun him. If that isn't effective, you'll separate from him.

"Hold on," you say. "Doesn't the wife have to continue to submit to her husband?"

No, she doesn't. Submission does not apply in these extraordinary circumstances. Where is submission in Matthew 18 and the other passages dealing with confronting sin? It's not there because when someone—a relative or a friend or your husband—is sinning, you don't submit to that person; you confront that person in the hope that he will turn from his sin.

Your husband has broken your marriage vows. He is severely damaging himself, you, and the children. A wife obeys the Lord before she obeys her husband. You would not submit to his robbing a bank or using pornography. You do not submit to a sinning husband. Not only has he sinned grievously against the Lord and his family, but he is failing to fulfill his biblical role as your loving, servant leader husband. What God wants you to do, and what the Bible teaches you to do, is to forget submission and go immediately into confrontation mode.

You don't submit to sin. You fight it. You resist it. According to the Bible, you shun the sinner until he genuinely repents and changes. Shunning means you do *nothing* for him, including having sex. To have sex with him now would be in the same category as rape. It would damage you emotionally, take a chunk out of your already critically wounded marriage, and push him farther into his sin. Plus, you put yourself at risk physically. Who knows what diseases he has picked up from his "lover"?

In Matthew 18:15–17 Jesus Christ presented the clear, powerful steps for dealing with a believer who is involved in willful, ongoing sin:

> If your brother sins against you, go and show him his fault, just between the two of you. If he listens to you, you have won your brother over. But if he will not listen, take one or two others along, so that "every matter may be established by the testimony of two or three witnesses." If he refuses to listen to them, tell it to the church; and if he refuses to listen even to the church, treat him as you would a pagan or a tax collector. (NIV)

These steps in Matthew 18 are the foundation of my approach to a spouse who wants out of a marriage. Whether he's having an affair or not, he is committing serious sins and needs to be confronted in the Matthew 18 way.

You talk to your husband in private. If he refuses to listen, you come back with one or two male friends or church leaders, and they talk to him. If he refuses to listen, you go directly to the elders (or other governing body) of your church and ask them to follow Scripture and tell the entire church what your husband is doing. In step two the meeting with you and your witnesses, your husband will be warned that telling the church is the next step.

If he still refuses to change after the local body of Christ is told of his sin, then you and everyone else in the church go into shunning mode. I've heard people laugh and joke about the Amish and their shunning. Let me tell you something. In this area they're right. They're following Scripture.

Jesus intends for you to take these Matthew 18 steps quickly and decisively. In Matthew 5:23–24 Jesus taught us that speed is important in handling grievances with others. If you're at the altar worshiping God and you realize there's something between you and a fellow believer, what do you do? Well, of course, you finish your spiritual time and then go to your brother. Wrong. Jesus said you are to leave the altar right away and go directly to your brother. That's pretty fast, isn't it?

It drives me crazy to hear or read pastors' and Christian authors' advice to spouses to "go slowly" and "not rush" when dealing with a sinning marriage partner. Do you honestly think Jesus would be in favor of stalling when it comes to sin? Hardly! Jesus wants you to move immediately to nip sin in the bud before it destroys any hope of saving the marriage. In the case of an affair, the sooner you move into confrontation mode, the better the chance that your husband will come to his senses and to God and stop what he is doing.

The longer you wait to do something, the deeper he plunges into the cesspool of sin. Any delay, any equivocation, is a signal to the adulterer that his sin can't be all that bad, or the fault is all or partly his wife's, and that an immediate, total separation from the woman in this illicit relationship is not necessary.

God has even provided us with a blueprint on how to handle serious sexual sin in the church. Paul devoted an entire chapter, 1 Corinthians 5, to describe how to deal with a fellow believer who was having sex with his mother (or stepmother). Using some of the strongest language in the New Testament, Paul followed the same basic set of instructions already laid down by Jesus as recorded by Matthew. He ordered the church members to "hand this man over to Satan" (1 Cor. 5:5 NIV) and kick him out of the local church immediately (1 Cor. 5:12–13). Paul stated that the Christians were to shun a Christian who was involved in sexual immorality or other serious sins (1 Cor. 5:9–11)!

SIN MUST BE CONFESSED

My use of the affair Document is unconventional, but it is also biblical. When I ask an adulterous husband to write out a detailed account of his affair and read it to his wife, what am I doing? I'm asking him to confess his sins, which is the same thing God asks him to do. Confession of sins is a central theme in the Old and New Testaments.

The Bible teaches us to confess our sins to God (Ps. 32:5; 1 John 1:9) and to one another (James 5:16). We are to go directly to the person we have harmed (Matt. 5:23–24) and speak in a completely honest and loving way (Eph. 4:15). Unconfessed sin is incredibly destructive and will eat a person alive (Ps. 32:3–4). Without a full and heartfelt confession, there is no brokenness or repentance or change.

Because of the seriousness and nature of adultery and because of what sex between human beings really is, saying "I'm sorry"—even if it is meant from the heart—is light-years away from being enough for the devastated spouse. Without true confession and repentance and restoration, no work for God or the spouse has begun.

FEELINGS MUST BE VENTED

I say it's very important for the victim of an affair to express her feelings directly to the adulterer again and again and again. Why? For two reasons. First, expression of painful feelings is biblical.

We're taught in Ephesians 4:26 to express whatever anger we feel each day. If we don't, we give Satan an opportunity to harass us. It's an opportunity he'll never miss exploiting.

We are to "carry each other's burdens" (Gal. 6:2 NIV). How can the adulterer carry his wife's burden unless she expresses to him what it is? It's a heavy, painful burden, so it will take months for her to express it sufficiently. Scripture places no limit on how long we are to carry a fellow believer's burden. We carry it—in this case, the husband carries it—as long as it takes that person to express it and heal from it, particularly when the husband is the cause of that crushing, debilitating burden.

If you want to read the world's greatest book of venting, read the psalms of David. David was not only the king of Israel. He was the king of the venters. In psalm after psalm, David poured out his feelings: anger, rage, feelings of helplessness, loneliness, fear, doubts, depression, deep hurt. David was perhaps closer to God than anyone else. If it was okay for David to express his feelings without limit or reservation, it's okay for the victim of an affair to do the same.

The second reason an affair victim must vent her pain is to promote healing and avoid personal destruction. This, of course, is why the Bible teaches that expression of feelings is necessary. If the victim doesn't fully vent, she will never forgive her husband fully. She will never trust him or any other man again. She will be a bitter, hostile woman. She'll be depressed and be susceptible to a broad range of physical disorders. Worst of all, she'll be spiritually dry. When I tell victims "vent or die," I'm not kidding.

RESTORATION IS THE GOAL

The ultimate goal of God's steps of discipline with a sinner is the same goal of my affair recovery program: restoration. God wants—and I want—the sinner to come back to his faith in obedience to Jesus and to blessed fellowship with Him. Back to his church. Back to his dear wife. Back to his family. But this restoration won't happen unless a tough love approach is used. There is a time for discipline and punishment (Heb. 12:6), and this is one of those critical times.

The perpetrator of the affair must be shaken to his roots. He is blind, arrogant, and temporarily out of his mind. He has chosen to walk away from God. He is firmly in the grip of Satan. He must be shown that he faces serious consequences in order to get his attention. A few taps with a pillow won't cut it. A determined, aggressive campaign against his sin-crazed brain might get the job done. In all this we must remember what sin is, what it does, that God hates it, and that it is the very reason God the Son had to die. To ever take sin lightly is to deny a cardinal doctrine of our faith.

I'm also committed to the restoration of the victim and her children. One of the reasons I use such a strong approach is to protect the kids. Jesus' words about the person who causes harm to children are harsh: "It would be better for him if, with a heavy millstone hung around his neck, he had been cast into the sea" (Mark 9:42). The adulterer is devastating his kids with his sinful behavior. He is destroying their security, trust, and self-esteem. All this when he should be bringing them up in "the discipline and instruction of the Lord" (Eph. 6:4). My approach provides the mom and the kids with security and strength as well as confirms the truth about right and wrong. It helps the shattered family heal, rebuild, and move on.

My program may not save the marriage, but I believe it is the only way that has the possibility of saving it. It will also get you and your precious children through the nightmare. Your husband may go down in a ball of flame, but he won't take you and the kids with him.

Is my program radical? Yes. Is it unorthodox? Yes. Is it extremely tough, even harsh? Yes. Is it a process that requires a lot of hard work from the adulterer and the victim? Yes. And does it provide respect and support and advocacy and healing for the victim? Yes. And here is the most important question: Is it true to the basic truths in the Bible? Yes.

THIRTEEN

FROM A DEAD MARRIAGE TO A BRAND-NEW LOVE

*The Stages of
Affair Recovery*

In terms of pain and devastation, adultery ranks right up there with the death of a loved one. It is betrayal and treachery of the highest order. Recovering from adultery takes time, an enormous amount of effort, and adherence to the right program.

Although each couple heals from adultery in a personal and unique way, in my experience most couples move through six stages of recovery. To help you understand these stages and give you an overview of the entire process, I'm going to show you how one couple—Dan and Debbie—worked their way from the discovery of adultery to a healthy, healed, and intimate marriage.

1. SHOCK AND DENIAL (TWO TO THREE WEEKS)

It was our first session, and Dan had just finished giving me a general description of his affair. Debbie had found out about the adultery eight days prior and was still in a state of shock. She couldn't yet fully grasp the reality that her rock solid, Christian husband had slept with another woman. Over the next few minutes, her comments to me confirmed that she wasn't getting it:

- "I can't believe Dan would do this."
- "This whole thing is like a terrible dream."
- "At least it lasted only two months."
- "If I'd only met his needs, he wouldn't have strayed."
- "I should have known; I should have seen the signs."
- "If we just look to the Lord and pray, everything will be fine."

With Dan sitting there, I told Debbie she was in shock and denial and needed to face the truth. Dan had committed adultery because he wanted to do it. He had made a terrible, selfish, and sinful choice, and it was 100 percent *his* fault. Dan's attitude was good in this opening session: he looked guilty, humble, and contrite. I gave him his instructions: end the affair with the final phone call, have no further contact with her, get the AIDS and STD tests, talk to his pastor and begin a spiritual growth and accountability program, and write the Document.

I gave Debbie her instructions: stop rationalizing, stop minimizing, stop blaming herself, and stop spiritualizing. I urged her to pray—by herself and with Dan—but not to expect prayer alone to heal the marriage. I shared my view that God would heal them by giving them the power to work the program. She needed to embrace the ugliness of what Dan had done and start getting angry. Very angry. I went over some of the how-to-get-angry techniques found in Chapter 6. As they left, I hoped and prayed Debbie would be able to get in touch with her anger.

2. RAGE (FOUR TO FIVE WEEKS)

Boy, did Debbie get in touch with her anger! She was angry even before Dan read his Document at the second session. After hearing him read the tawdry details of his adultery, she went beyond anger and turned into an erupting volcano of rage. I gave Debbie permission to open up and let the rage out. I told Dan to hunker down and take it like a man. He deserved everything he was going to get, and he needed to handle Debbie's rage with patience and kindness.

Over the next month or so, Debbie pummeled Dan with her rage. Her Document of Response was ten full pages of fury, anguish, and disgust. Every night, after the kids were in bed, she launched into a verbal assault of vented emotions and specific questions. Their sessions often lasted well into the early morning hours.

I explained to Dan what Debbie was doing in the verbal beatings. First, she was flushing out her emotions so she could heal and eventually forgive him. Second, she was punishing him. Simply put, she wanted revenge. She wanted him to suffer in at least a tiny fraction of the way he caused her to suffer. Finally, she was testing him to find out if he really loved her and was committed to her. Did he accept the gravity of his sin, and did he love her enough and want to save the marriage enough to take this punishment?

Debbie tested Dan by throwing everything *and* the kitchen sink at him. She cornered him and forced him into no-win situations time and time again. She asked loaded questions and blasted him no matter how he responded. If he told the truth, she was furious because the truth hurt so much. If he paused, she accused him of stalling to think up a story. If he gave a slightly different answer to a question she'd asked before, she called him a liar.

I taught Dan that the way he responded to Debbie's almost constant barrage of feelings of pain and questions was essential to the healing process. I urged him not to get impatient, lash back, cut her off, shut down, or leave the intense conversations. To do any of these behaviors would hurt her *again* and prove his lack of love for her.

Dan called me once and complained, "Dave, she's trying to get me to lose my temper and give up!"

I replied, "You're exactly right. Hang in there, and you'll have the best chance to win her back. If she runs you over with a tank one thousand times, don't react. Get up one thousand times and come back for more. You hurt her terribly, and now you have to help her recover. She has to know and feel you love her before she can forgive you and give her heart back to you."

To Dan's credit, he stepped up and got the job done. He asked Debbie every day if she wanted to talk about his affair. He listened and reflected back her emotions. He worked hard to walk in her shoes and feel her pain. He patiently answered all her questions day after day after day. He said he was sorry a million times. When he made mistakes with careless responses or defensive reactions, impatience, or small acts of selfishness, he apologized and got right back into The Mode. He was kind and loving in the face of Debbie's rage, meanness, sarcasm, and brutal rejection.

Even though Debbie did not seem to be responding too well or giving him any encouragement, Dan was making important changes. He respected Debbie again. He loved her again. He began responding to her needs. He traded his car because he and the paramour had sex in it. He gave to charity all the clothes he had worn during his trysts with the adulteress. He was prepared to leave his job because she was a coworker, but stayed when she left. I told him that was God's reward for his doing a good job in the recovery process.

Dan had his AIDS and STD tests done, and they came back negative. He found a strong, spiritual Christian man to be his once-a-week accountability partner. He joined a small group of men at their church for discipleship and spiritual growth. Dan did not know Jesus Christ personally, but he began to consider the claims of Jesus. He attended church services, and he read his Bible faithfully in preparation for his meetings with his mentor and the group. At first, he did these things to please Debbie. But as time went on, I got the impression that he was serious about his spiritual status.

When Debbie questioned Dan's sincerity, I said, "Hey, I don't blame you for being skeptical. However, he's putting a lot of effort into this process. Let's just wait and see what happens. Time will tell."

3. THE HONEYMOON (ONE TO TWO WEEKS)

After about one month of raging at Dan, Debbie suddenly softened one night. Instead of the usual seek-and-destroy mission in the family room, she took his hand and said she loved him. She said that she was beginning to believe he did love her and that they could make it. She kissed him passionately. She kissed him some more. She asked him if he wanted to have sex. Fortunately, Dan didn't faint dead away. He couldn't say yes fast enough, and they had intercourse for the first time in six weeks.

When Dan and Debbie told me the good news at our next session, I told them that what was happening was a positive sign that they were making solid progress. I explained that they were now in a brief but important stage called the honeymoon. Since they had both done their recovery jobs well so far, romantic love and passion would reenter their relationship.

They would be given a brief hiatus from the difficult, painful parts of the recovery process. They would reconnect as a couple both physically and emotionally. They would find each other as a couple again and feel hope that they could restore their marriage.

I said that they needed the honeymoon and that it would be intense and wonderful. I also said it wouldn't last long, but they should enjoy it.

I informed Dan and Debbie that about 80 percent of the couples I'd seen in recovery from adultery went through the honeymoon. It is not a stage experienced by all couples. If a couple had a very strained marriage for years and never really developed a deep love for each other, they won't get the honeymoon. If a couple is having a difficult recovery process and struggling to follow my program, they won't get the honeymoon. If these couples hang in there and work hard, they get their honeymoon at the end of the process.

Dan and Debbie's honeymoon lasted two weeks. They cuddled. They made out. They had intercourse at least every other day. They laughed together. They played together. They talked about positive, uplifting topics. They prayed together. They dreamed about the future together. They took a few weekend trips together without the kids. And then one night, Debbie cried after sex, and the honeymoon was over. Poof! The really hard work was about to begin.

4. ANGER (THREE TO FOUR WEEKS)

Just after the honeymoon ended with a thud, Dan and Debbie were in my office. Debbie was furious—again—and Dan was discouraged. I told them that they were entering the Anger Stage and it wouldn't be pretty. It was time to get back to work. I described what they would go through. And sure enough, they did.

Over the next three weeks, Debbie's anger roared back. It wasn't the white-hot fury of the Rage Stage, but a cold and calculating anger. She went back to the daily venting of her emotions. She went back to the questioning. She went back to the biting sarcasm and ridicule. To Dan's dismay, she did not go back to even a drop of human kindness, affection, or romance.

I told Dan privately that Debbie would be an absolute witch for three or four weeks, maybe longer. His job was to maintain patience, kindness, and love in the midst of Hurricane Debbie. As with all honeymoons, their honeymoon was the eye of the hurricane, and the eye had passed. Debbie was putting him through a final testing. She needed to know if she could be vulnerable with him and trust him with her life and her deeper feelings.

In the Anger Stage Debbie broadened her attacks from Dan's adultery to everything else he'd ever done to hurt her in the marriage. With the memory of an elephant and the approach of a charging rhinoceros, Debbie went after everything the man had ever done wrong. Every hurt. Every dumb mistake. Every careless action. Every weakness. She brought up his business practices, his lost promotions, his weight, his bad breath, his shortcomings as a father, the way he picked his teeth after meals, the time he spent on the computer. Dan told me it was like having his life flash before his eyes just before dying except he saw only the negative things—and he wasn't going to be allowed to die.

Overreactions and emotional scenes were the order of the day. Debbie would mention one of his weaknesses, magnify it out of all proportion, and rail at him for thirty minutes. Then she would say she was going to divorce him. Or she'd ask him to leave the home. Or she'd say if he were a real man, he'd divorce her. He'd start to pack a bag because she told him to, and she'd say, "What are you doing? I don't want you to go." And then he'd have to endure thirty more minutes of anger about what a quitter he was.

In Debbie's eyes Dan was a pitiful loser who couldn't do anything right. She asked him to go on a diet with her, and he agreed. The diet was a nightmare for him. If he didn't lose enough weight, he was fat and lazy and obviously not committed to her. If he lost more weight than she lost, she accused him of trying to make her feel bad.

Debbie went back to the detective mode. She had checked up on him in the Rage Stage but not this frequently and intensely. She called him unpredictably during the day to ask him where he was, what he had done up to that point, whether he'd talked to the woman with whom he had the affair, what he was doing now, and what his plans were for the rest of the day. She drove by his office to make sure his car was there. Just about every day, she checked his briefcase, his appointment book, his car, his cell phone, and his computer.

She tested him again and again in a variety of ways. She forced him to tell her when he'd be home after work, and if he was one minute late and hadn't called, she would take his head off. Even if he had called to tell her why he'd be delayed, she'd still take his head off. She'd wake him up at two in the morning and want to talk, and if he was the slightest bit annoyed or reluctant, she'd blast him with a verbal barrage.

Debbie did a lot of the same testing behaviors she'd done back in the Rage Stage, but now actually did more of them and used a higher level of creativity. One day, for example, she put a lingerie company catalog on the coffee table with a pen on it at a certain place and angle. That way, she would know if Dan had looked at it. Fortunately for Dan, he didn't go near it. Of course, Debbie wondered if he was just clever enough to replace the pen in exactly the same way she placed it.

Debbie verbalized a number of thoughts and feelings that are very common in this stage:

- "How can I stay married to a man who has committed adultery?"
- "I can't ever trust him again!"
- "I shouldn't have to be going through all this!"
- "He'll sleep with another woman—I know it!"
- "Why should I give my heart back to him only to have him rip it apart again?"
- "I'd be a fool to stay with him!"
- "I think I'll have an affair of my own. That will show him!"
- "I have a biblical reason to divorce him."

I told Dan and Debbie that these statements were all quite normal. The thought of divorce and living alone was protective for Debbie because she still wasn't 100 percent positive that Dan would genuinely change. Considering life on her own was also empowering for her. She needed to know that she was strong enough to make it by herself if she believed Dan's behavior and attitude made it necessary. I continued to hold firm to my belief that, with God's help, they could restore their marriage. I stressed that Dan's continued ability to take her hits and remain comforting and loving would eventually convince Debbie to stay in the new marriage.

Dan wasn't the only one with whom Debbie was angry. In a private session with me, she did some serious venting and questioning about God's part in this:

- "I'm furious with God for allowing this pain in my life!"
- "Why would God allow the adultery?"
- "Is God punishing me?"

- "Why didn't God step in and stop it?"

- "Why didn't God reveal the affair to me before they had sex?"

- "I was a good Christian, and look what happened."

Debbie felt guilty for these questions that seemed to indicate a lack of faith in the Lord. She was worried that her issues with God would drive Dan farther away from Him. I urged her to continue expressing these feelings, directly to God her Father and with one or two close female Christian friends. I told her that her feelings and doubts concerning God were perfectly normal. She had plenty of godly company in the Bible in the area of wrestling with God: Job, Jeremiah, David, and Paul, to mention a few. I assured her that she'd come through her doubts with a stronger, deeper faith. I also said it was okay to be honest with Dan about her spiritual issues. He might as well see how believers' faith operates and is tested in the real world.

5. Depression (Four to Six Weeks)

Debbie's anger finally began to subside, and in its place came depression. There were still pockets of anger she expressed from time to time, but the terrible hurt that Dan had caused her became her predominant feeling. She got in touch with the deep sadness and grief connected to Dan's adultery. She felt like a firefighter who, having battled a raging wildfire for weeks, was now able to survey the devastation.

Dan had broken a solemn, sacred promise. He had defiled and destroyed their marriage. He had taken something precious, eminently private and special, a wonderful gift God bestowed, something intended only for her, and had given it to someone else. He had insulted her and shown her disrespect and completely rejected her. He had shattered her trust in him. He had wounded her in the most personal, private way imaginable. Dan had deliberately thrown away—irretrievably—something of inestimable value to Debbie (and to any spouse, perhaps particularly a woman).

Debbie needed time and space to grieve all these losses. For several weeks, she pulled away from Dan and didn't have much to say to him. She went to a motel over two consecutive weekends to think, to pray, and to weep. To grieve. She worked things out with God and renewed her fellowship with Him. She expressed her hurt and pain with two very close friends.

With my urging, Debbie opened up to Dan and shared her hurt and sadness. It was a risk to be so vulnerable, but it was a good risk because Dan had done well in the recovery process. Both of them told me this stage was harder and more painful than either Rage or Anger.

When Dan saw Debbie's broken heart, his heart was broken. He could clearly see and feel, for the first time, what his sin had done to his dear wife. He did his best to comfort her, often holding her without speaking for hours at a time. His tenderness and understanding touched Debbie and helped her heal and feel closer to him.

Dan did a searching self-examination and found out why he committed adultery. He concentrated on changing because he realized the "old Dan" and his "old behavior" would always remind Debbie of his affair. He worked hard on his weaknesses as a man, as a husband, as a father, and as a child of God.

One major change was learning how to do something he could never do before with Debbie: communicate. By following my recovery program, he learned how to talk to her openly and express his emotions. How to listen and reflect. How to handle conflict without walking away or losing his temper. How to emotionally connect with Debbie.

The greatest change was in the spiritual area. Going to church regularly, attending his small discipleship/accountability group, being accountable to one spiritual man, and reading the Bible all combined to make Dan aware he needed God in his life. One day, in a meeting with the pastor, he accepted the good news about Jesus Christ. He believed Jesus died for all his sins and rose from the dead. Dan trusted what Jesus had done for him and so began a relationship with the living God.

During the last part of the Depression Stage, Debbie took a good, hard look at herself and her weaknesses. She had been a passive, unassertive person with a poor self-image. She had allowed Dan to control and even mistreat her. But no more. She had been just a wife and a mom, with no clearly defined sense of self or of what God wanted her to do with her gifts and talents. But no more.

Debbie cleaned out past pain from her family, especially in her relationship with her dad. With Dan's encouragement and support, she wrote her dad a long, honest letter and sent it. In therapy she talked through some major mistakes she'd made in her life. Doing this brought her the experience of God's forgiveness and emotional wholeness. Her work in my program and this extra work helped her become an assertive, self-confident person who knew what *she* could do as a person for God.

Debbie felt her love for Dan returning. Romance, affection, and sex began again. At times, after intercourse, Debbie would feel too vulnerable and pull back from Dan for a day or two. Then, she'd come back to him.

6. REBUILDING THE MARRIAGE (SIX TO EIGHT WEEKS)

Dan and Debbie were 80 to 85 percent healed from his adultery. They had done a lot of good, solid work on themselves as individuals and on their relationship. Now it was time to focus on their marriage and make all the changes necessary for a healthy, loving bond.

We worked on communicating. Handling conflict. Meeting needs. Understanding male-female differences. Having a healthy sex life. Parenting. Dealing with finances. Creating a spiritual bond as a couple (as I describe in my book *A Marriage After God's Own Heart*). Because of all the changes they'd already made in the recovery process, this work wasn't that difficult. Because they had talked and talked about the most difficult and personal issues conceivable, they could now talk about anything.

They were open. They were honest. They admitted faults. They compromised. Over the almost six months I saw Dan and Debbie in therapy, they made tremendous progress. As with most couples I've taken through my recovery from adultery program, it took another six months for them to completely heal. When I released them from therapy, I told them to keep doing what they were doing, and in six months they'd be healed.

I got a call six months later, and Dan and Debbie told me that they had continued the steps we'd begun and their marriage was "terrific." They had bought new wedding rings, and they invited me to a ceremony where they would renew their wedding vows. I attended the event and shared in their joy. Those are my favorite kinds of wedding ceremonies.

If Dan and Debbie can make it, you and your spouse can make it. God can take something broken—from a human standpoint hopeless—and make it into something beautiful. If you follow the program and do the work required, you can go from zero respect to 100 percent respect. From zero trust to 100 percent trust. From zero forgiveness to 100 percent forgiveness. From zero intimacy to 100 percent intimacy. From a dead marriage to a brand-new love.

FOURTEEN

QUESTIONS
AND ANSWERS

*Common Questions About
Recovery from Adultery*

Q: *Your approach and tone in this book are harsh, blunt, and
aggressive. Why?*

A: I use an extremely tough, no-nonsense tone with my
therapy clients and with readers of this book for some very
good reasons. First, my approach comes from the way that
the Bible states we are to deal with someone who is
involved in serious sin. The tone used in passage after
passage is tough as nails: 2 Corinthians 13; 2 Samuel 12;
2 Thessalonians 3; Titus 3; 1 Corinthians 5; and Matthew 18.
The Old Testament unequivocally labels adultery as
heinous: Exodus 20:14, repeated in Deuteronomy 5:18 (a
list of the Ten Commandments); Leviticus 20:10; and
Proverbs 5. Israel's choosing other gods—idolatry, the
worst sin of all—is called "adultery," contamination, by the
true God. God invented tough love, and He wants us to
use it to save a life from the consequences of sin.
Second, I'm exhorting victims of adultery to take
dramatic, difficult actions *quickly.* Exhortation is not nice,

sweet, and gentle. It is in-your-face, abrasive, drill sergeant tough. I'm motivating and pushing victims to see the truth and get angry enough to do something about it. I'm lighting a fire under them to get them past denial and into a program that can save their marriages.

When there's an explosion on board a ship and water is rushing in, a good captain moves swiftly and aggressively to assess and repair the damage. He doesn't concern himself with kindness and proper etiquette. He doesn't worry about hurting anyone's feelings. He barks out orders to save the ship. When a tumor threatens to take a life, the surgeon cuts right into the body, regardless of inevitable pain, to remove it. God does the same: "The LORD . . . heals the bruise He has inflicted" (Isa. 30:26); and "He has torn us, but He will heal us; He has wounded us, but He will bandage us" (Hos. 6:1).

Third, my program is exactly what is required to drag a sinning spouse from Satan's grip. James 4:7 and 1 Peter 5:8–9 teach us to "resist the devil" because he is "like a roaring lion" on the prowl, "seeking someone to devour." In Ephesians 6:10–18 Paul told us that we are in a spiritual battle. This is never more true than when your spouse is deceived into believing his sin is okay. You've got to hit him hard and fast in this battle for his soul and your marriage. You've got to smash him to shake him loose from this supernatural, incredibly powerful, spiritual foe.

Fourth, my "crowbar to the adulterer's head" strategy (metaphorically speaking, of course) has the best chance to create genuine brokenness. Think about the word *broken*. You have to hit something—or someone—hard in order to break it. If you don't get brokenness, you won't get genuine sorrow over sin and repentance.

Finally, you can afford to lighten up and gradually become warm and kind when your sinning spouse truly repents, makes important changes, and proves the changes over time. Second Corinthians 2:5–10 teaches us to forgive and restore to fellowship a sinner who repents. I'm very tough on the adulterer at first. As he or she works the program and turns back to God and spouse, I become a pretty nice guy. Many perpetrators of adultery have later thanked me for being so hard-nosed because that was what they needed.

In the event your spouse doesn't repent and change, you still have to forgive. The Bible teaches us to forgive others whether they are repentant or not (Matt. 6:12, 14–15). If you don't forgive, your bitterness and resentment will eat you alive. Plus, your failure to forgive will drive a wedge between you and God.

A reconciliation, however, is a completely different matter. With a caring pastor or Christian therapist, you'll work through the stages of trauma and forgive your spouse. But you will not work on the marriage or reconcile until your spouse has changed.

Q: *Won't your recovery program scare my spouse off?*

A: It's very possible. If it does, there's your answer. If he will not follow the plan, do you really want him back? That is a very serious question for you to answer—logically, realistically. I'm not interested in some kind of halfhearted, half-baked patch job. This is a quantum leap from requiring only a Band-Aid. I want and God wants—and you'd better want—real change. Keep in mind that you can't scare someone off who's already gone. The only question is, Will he stay gone or come back to you? Besides, someone who truly loves you cannot be scared off.

You must push the adulterer to make a choice he'll avoid unless you force it. He won't choose to take the right steps unless you insist, and you shouldn't want restoration on any other terms.

Q: *Won't your recovery plan push him back to the other woman?*

A: He's already with the other woman—if not physically, certainly emotionally. My program gives you the best shot at prying him loose from her. If he comes back to the marriage on easy terms, he's not back at all. He's still just as much with the other woman, only in a very unhealthy, dangerous way for the wife.

Q: *Won't your program make my spouse very depressed?*

A: We can hope so. He needs to be depressed, so he'll break and repent. Nathan didn't seem too worried about depressing David when he drilled the king with God's message in 2 Samuel. The pain of grieving over his sin will move him to repentance and closer to God and to you (see again 2 Cor. 7:9–10). That's good, healthy depression. If he stays in the affair or doesn't recover from it and keeps pining away for the other woman, he'll eventually be overwhelmed with pain and grief. That's bad, sinful depression.

Q: *How do you explain couples who seem to recover from affairs without dealing with it your way? They don't talk about it much; they just move past it and look happy.*

A: "Seem to recover" is the key. They might appear to have recovered, but under the surface they haven't. The adultery remains a festering wound that is damaging each of them and the marriage, and if left this way, it will always have a damaging, destructive effect. The victim has not won back any respect and lives in a state of fear and distrust and unforgivingness. The adulterer still has the paramour in his heart and is more likely to commit adultery again. If they look happy, it's only superficial. They're working hard to stay in denial, but this doesn't change their hearts or their souls.

Q: *What if the affair wasn't physical but only emotional? Do we still have to follow your recovery plan?*

A: Yes, you do. An "only emotional" affair is, in my opinion, a full-blown affair and must be treated as such. If there was no physical contact, you still must work through every step of my program.

Q: *If I had an affair years ago and my spouse doesn't know, do I need to tell him or her?*

A: Yes, you do. And the sooner, the better. Unconfessed sin of this magnitude wreaks havoc on a marriage. It will always be between the two of you, pulling you apart week by week, month by month, year by year. The guilt and shame that you—the adulterer—carry will prevent you from being open and intimate with your mate. Your secret sin will give Satan a foothold in your life and marriage. Follow the Bible (Matt. 5:23–24; James 5:16) and confess your sin. If both spouses have had affairs, both must confess their sin. Then, both must follow all my steps of recovery at the same time.

Q: *I'm just not strong enough to take the steps you want me to take with my adulterous spouse. I want to, but I can't. What do you suggest?*

A: You're not strong enough on your own. No one is. You need help and support. Get a solid group of family and friends to encourage you, uplift you, and exhort you to be aggressive. There is strength in numbers. Find a tough-minded therapist who will guide you through the process. Ask your pastor and church leaders for assistance. Reread Chapters 4, 5, and 6 of this book. Cling to God and ask Him for the power you need to act.

Q: *Look, I've made a lot of mistakes and feel that I drove my spouse to have the affair. Because I feel partly responsible for the adultery, how can I be as tough as you're asking me to be?*

A: Does anyone believe that any failure or weakness on the part of a spouse justifies adultery on the part of the other? The only issue now is your spouse's adultery. You can't deal with the adultery and the marital issues at the same time. If you take any responsibility *at all* for the adultery, your spouse will not genuinely be broken, and your marriage won't heal. The affair is 100 percent your partner's fault, it must stop, and you must *first* go through the recovery from adultery steps.

Admit your mistakes openly and agree you are at least 50 percent at fault for *the marital problems*. However, you do not open up and deal with your mistakes in the marriage until you know your spouse has stopped the affair, loves you again, and is well on his way to changing. Say to your adulterous spouse: "You first, then me."

Q: *What do you think about special "spiritual healing" ceremonies for adultery? Will a healing-of-memories experience in which my pain is given to Jesus help us recover?*

A: This kind of experience can certainly help, but it won't completely heal you from the trauma of adultery. God will heal you and restore your marriage through the difficult, painful steps of recovery I've described. From a spiritual, an emotional, even an intellectual standpoint, I have explained the path to healing. There is no shortcut or way around it.

Q: *Who should I tell about my spouse's affair?*

A: I urge you to tell the entire story to several very close, trusted, solid Christian friends. Even if your spouse is repentant and doing everything right to help you heal, you need support. You can't bear the burden alone (Gal. 6:2), and it's important for others to pray specifically for you and your spouse (Matt. 18:19–20).

If your spouse is following my program and you see the right attitude in him, you don't have to tell your family about the adultery. It's not wrong to tell them, and you can if you need to, but understand it will complicate his reconciliation with your relatives. I do recommend you tell your family you are having marital problems because you need their encouragement and prayers.

If your husband has a bad attitude and is resisting my recovery program, tell your family everything. Tell his family everything. Tell his friends everything. Ask his family and friends to confront him and take a tough love stand against his sin. Make it clear you expect them to follow Scripture, and cut him off if he chooses to continue in his sin.

Because we are talking about *adultery,* you *do* ask others to take sides—that's what the Bible teaches. You're going to find out in a hurry who your real friends are. Those who refuse are no friends of yours. They are wimps. Worse, they are sinning by disobeying Scripture and enabling your spouse's sin. There will always be those around you who believe saving the marriage is all that matters, and they will consider ignoring, or going easy on the adultery, a price worth paying. Pull back from these persons.

Go to your pastor and church leaders and ask them to follow Matthew 18:15–17 and apply church discipline if necessary. If they refuse, leave your church and find a church whose leaders obey the Bible. If you're strong enough, ask several friends to confront your church leaders as indicated in Matthew 18. Being faced by others urging the same biblical steps they're refusing to follow may convict them of their sin.

Q: *If my spouse is genuinely broken and really working to win me back, do we still need to dredge up the past and follow your program?*

A: Yes. If you want to get 100 percent trust, 100 percent respect, 100 percent change, and 100 percent healing, you need to do 100 percent of my program. Don't take any chances. Seize this moment to make sure your spouse changes and won't ever do this to you again.

Q: *My spouse is repentant, and we're following your recovery program. Do we still need to tell the kids something?*

A: Yes, but only in general terms. Since your spouse is on the right track, you don't need to bring up the adultery. The two of you need to gather your children and tell them that Mom and Dad are having marriage problems. Tell them that you are working on them and, with God's help, you hope to solve the problems. Then pray out loud that

God will help you both to rebuild your marriage and give all of you strength and peace and victory. Ask the children to pray for Mom and Dad when they talk to God.

If someone else tells your children about the affair, you'll have no choice but to tell them the truth. Make your explanation very general and give no details.

Q: *How do we get the time to talk through the adultery?*

A: You make the time. Especially in the first three to four months, you need time each day to talk privately. You need to do your recovery work now—right now. With the exception of work and children, clear everything else from your calendars. Drop church jobs. Say no to social engagements. In fact, temporarily halt your social lives. People may wonder what's going on. Let them wonder. Do not let relatives and friends come and visit during this recovery time. Not even for a few days. These people will be disappointed. Tough.

Put the kids in their bedrooms early so you can talk. Or drop them off at a friend's home for a few hours. Lean heavily on family and friends to take your kids—during the week and for at least several weekends.

Q: *My husband's paramour is pregnant. What do we do about the child?*

A: As bad as it is that this child will not have a relationship with his biological father, make it clear to your husband that he will have no contact of any kind with this child. Ever. The child is a constant reminder of his adultery. Seeing the child means seeing the mother, however briefly. Every contact will rip open your wound and keep you from healing. If a blood test proves your husband is the father, you will have to provide monthly support. But that's all you'll provide.

Q: *My husband's affair was with a friend of ours. The two families have spent a lot of time together, and my kids are good friends with the other person's kids. What can I do?*

A: You have no choice but to cut off all contact between the families. You must get as far away from the other woman as possible. Her kids will remind you of her and the adultery. Plus, you don't want your kids exposed to the person who betrayed and hurt you so heartlessly. Tell your children a serious conflict has come up, and while you are very sorry, this has caused Mom and Dad to decide to sever all ties with this family. Your kids won't like it or fully understand it, but they'll adjust.

Q: *My husband told me he can't stand the stress of all the demands I've put on him as a result of his affair. He has threatened to kill himself. What do you suggest?*

A: Tell him that his stress is coming from his sin and his unwillingness to fully break and follow the program. Chances are very good, he's trying to manipulate you into backing off. Say to him, "Just be sure you don't make a mess in the home. Gas up the car, get your life insurance all paid up, and put your financial affairs in order."

If you think he's serious about ending his life, call his bluff and contact the police. If they assess him and think he's suicidal, they'll take him to the hospital. And on a serious note, be aware that no one ever makes another person take his life. That is a choice only the suicide makes, and very often it is—in error, of course—an attempt to cast guilt on survivors. Don't ever accept that responsibility.

*Q: My adulterous spouse wants me to agree to a financial
settlement right away so we can avoid high attorney fees. I think
if I'm nice about this divorce process, he may change his mind
and come back to me.*

A: Sinful, selfish persons don't come back to doormats. They
only wipe their feet on them. Don't agree to a divorce.
Don't sign any financial settlement agreement that only
he and his attorney have cooked up. He wants a quick
divorce so he can keep most of his money and legitimize
his adultery.

Tell him to go ahead and file for divorce from you if
that is what he wants to do. Let him know you will hire
your own attorney and fight him for every last cent you
can get. If you are living in a state where his adultery can
be used against him legally, that's exactly what you'll do.

Q: Should I tell the paramour's spouse about the affair?

A: If the other victimized spouse is a friend, a family
member, or a fellow Christian, the answer is yes. If you
don't know the person, it's a judgment call. You don't
have to, but I usually recommend that my clients do tell.
It's a public service. You'd want to be told, wouldn't you?

If the other spouse is a stranger, make a brief phone
call and stay anonymous. You don't need some homicidal
maniac on your tail on top of your already stressful
situation.

If you think your spouse is lying to you about how
serious the affair was, it can be a good idea to call the
other spouse to compare notes and gather information.
Don't meet in person; just use the phone. Don't develop
any kind of relationship with this person—all you want is
information.

Q: *My spouse is doing all he can to help me heal from his adultery. His attitude is great, and he has followed all your steps of recovery. But I'm still stuck and cannot seem to move past what he has done to me. Any suggestions?*

A: It's very easy to get stuck in the recovery process. Here are some ideas that may help:

- Schedule two or three individual sessions with your therapist. Look at your past unresolved pain because it's probably transferring to the current pain of the adultery, thus compounding it.

- Make sure you've not skipped the Anger Stage. You need to completely vent your anger, or you'll get mired in depression.

- Write another letter to your spouse. Ask the Lord to enable you to identify and express all the pain that's still inside. Focus on your sadness and hurt.

- Write a letter to God about your spouse's adultery and its impact on you. If you're still angry at God, tell Him. He can take it. Tell Him you're releasing your pain to Him.

- If you're still resentful of friends who knew about the affair and didn't tell you, write letters and send them.

- Write a letter to the other woman expressing your feelings about her role in harming you and your family. Don't send it, of course. You'll forgive her, but there will be no relationship with her.

- Ask your support team to pray that you will be able to forgive your spouse and move past his terrible sin.

- Pray with support team members on the phone and in person. Ask them to catch you when you obsess about the adultery.

- Fight your negative, irrational thoughts, and work to replace them with positive, realistic thoughts. Write down on a three-by-five card the good, solid changes your spouse has made, and carry it with you.

- Begin or continue a regular, vigorous exercise program.

- Spend time daily in prayer and read the Bible and/or devotional materials.

- Risk being open and vulnerable again with your spouse. Take small, baby steps in affection and romance and communication. It's okay to start and then stop for a day or two. Just start again.

Q: *Should I ask my adulterous spouse to read your book?*

A: Yes. It's a good idea. It will give him insight into how much pain he has caused in your life. And it will teach him exactly what he has to do and why. Ask him to read the book only after he's broken and is ready to do whatever it takes to win you back. In fact, at this point make it one of the requirements.

If he says, "You know I hate to read," you can be sure he's not broken yet. A humble, broken man will read the dictionary if you ask, and he will do it gladly.

Q: *Dave, I just don't know if we can make it. Even if my spouse does everything right and we follow your program, how can I ever trust him again? How can our marriage ever be the same as it was?*

A: It's a God thing. God created man and woman and
   marriage, and only He can give any of us a good marriage,
   let alone repair a damaged one. God alone can give you the
   strength to follow the program. God alone can help both of
   you change. God alone can restore your marriage and give
   you back respect, trust, and intimacy. Your marriage won't
   ever be the same. With hard work and God's power, it will
   be better. Ephesians 3:20 (NIV) sums it up: "Now to him
   who is able to do immeasurably more than all we ask or
   imagine, according to his power that is at work within us."

PART 3

"I DON'T LOVE YOU, AND I'M NOT HAVING AN AFFAIR"

FIFTEEN

LIVING IN
A LOVELESS MARRIAGE

It's Not Adultery,
But It's Still Serious Sin

You are confident your spouse is not having an affair. That's the good news. The bad news is he doesn't love you. Maybe he has said the words, "I don't love you anymore." Maybe he hasn't. But his behavior sends that message loud and clear.

He is a lousy husband. He is selfish. He doesn't meet your needs. He won't romance you. He won't make time to be with you. He won't talk to you on a personal level. He won't listen to you when you want to share your thoughts and feelings. He won't be your spiritual leader. He mistreats you. He may even abuse you physically and/or emotionally. He has at least one sinful, destructive behavior pattern that he will not stop. And this behavior pattern is causing him to mistreat you and to not love you.

RECOGNIZING A "BAD HUSBAND" MARRIAGE

I'm going to briefly describe several "bad husband" marriages. These are all real cases that I saw in therapy. I could tell you hundreds of similar stories because marriages like these are very common. Although I'm focusing on husbands, there are plenty of wives who could be the problem in each scenario.

Mr. Lazy

Jim reminded me of a little boy who never grew up. He had completed college but could not seem to find a stable career. He went from job to job, never staying longer than a year or two. He blamed his bosses for each firing, but the truth was, he didn't work hard enough. He was just plain lazy. He'd show up for work late and put in very little effort. He spent money irresponsibly and ran up large credit card bills. His wife, Carol, was forced to work at a job she didn't like in order to make ends meet. She was burdened by their debt, but Jim didn't seem to be concerned.

The Workaholic

Bob sat quietly as his wife, Pam, talked about his job and how consuming it was. She told me he left early each morning before anyone else was up. He got home late and spent very little time with her and the kids. In fact, most evenings he continued to work on the phone and the computer. He worked weekends and missed many church and school events. Bob denied he was a workaholic and said he had to work to meet the needs of his family.

The Sex Addict

Through her sobs, Janet told me her husband, Steve, had a problem with pornography. Over the last ten years, she'd caught him four times viewing pornography: once, a television program; once, an X-rated video; and twice, Internet sites. Each time he said that he was sorry and that it wouldn't happen again. But he refused to seek counseling help and would not tell her all he had done in the sexual area. He told her it was no big deal and all guys did it. It didn't hurt anyone. He was not interested in her sexually. They had sex, on average, once every two months. She had just recently discovered that, over the past six months, Steve had visited more than fifty pornographic Web sites.

The Alcoholic

Larry admitted to me that he liked to drink. He had a few beers after work and drank more on the weekends. "I mean," he said with a smile, "what's a ball game without a few cold ones?" His wife, Susan, was not smiling and told me she was very upset by Larry's drinking. She said he was different when he drank: sloppy, loud, rude, and irritable. She told me he loved the beer more than he loved her. Larry refused to accept the truth that he was an alcoholic and told Susan she was "a bad housekeeper and a nag." He was convinced Susan didn't like his drinking because her father had been a drunk. He insisted he was just a social drinker and didn't need to give up alcohol.

Mr. Mouth

In their first session together, Mike admitted he had a temper. He said he'd "get angry, blow up, and then get over it quickly." Shawna, with some prodding from me, described a verbally abusive man with a volatile, unpredictable temper. Some days, he was fine. Other days, he'd be in a bad mood, and anything could set him off. He would yell, use profanity, and be sarcastic and belittling. Sometimes, he'd punch the wall or throw things. His rage could be directed at her or one of the kids. He had never hit anyone, but the emotional damage was significant. Mike, to no one's surprise, got angry at Shawna's description, and in a loud voice he said he didn't lose his temper that often, and when he did, it was for good reasons.

The Violent Man

Sharon, in a voice just above a whisper, confided in me that Bill hit her about once every three months. It was the same cycle every time: his stress would build up, he'd get edgy and irritable, they'd start arguing, he'd slap her or shove her, then he'd be very sorry and promise never to hit her again. He'd be nice and loving to her for about a month, then his stress would begin building.

This had been going on for seven years, and now that the kids were older, Sharon was worried they would be affected by the violence. Bill thought all psychologists were "quacks" and forbade her to tell anyone about *her* problem or what she considered to be the problem. He accused her of baiting him and forcing him to explode.

The Controller

Denise told me her husband, Frank, had asked her to see a therapist to "get your head on straight and stop being depressed all the time." I saw very quickly why Denise was depressed. Frank controlled every area of her life and their marriage. He handled all the money and told her nothing about what he did with it. He gave her an allowance each month to spend on groceries, the kids, and gas. He wanted his meals on time, no laundry left in the dryer, and the house kept neat as a pin. He wanted her to replace the soap when it got too small. He accused her of spending too much money, but he spent money freely on things he wanted. Everything that went wrong was always her fault. If she displeased him, he'd ignore her for days. If she ever dared speak up, he'd threaten to divorce her. His emotional abuse was ripping her emotional health to shreds.

Do any of these case studies sound familiar? Many of you reading these words are living in one of these nightmare marriages.

He's not having an affair, but his behavior is killing your marriage. Adultery destroys a marriage quickly. These destructive behavior patterns I've described slowly eat away at a marriage. But in the end, the marriage is just as dead.

Stop kidding yourself. Your husband doesn't love you. He hasn't loved you for some time. *And he's not going to start loving you unless you do something about his disgraceful, sinful behavior.*

"BUT DON'T I HAVE TO SUBMIT?"

All of these wives told me they had come to me as a last resort. Each had sought help from a variety of Christian sources: marriage books, pastors, counselors, and friends. They had received the same, basic message from these "helpers":

> There isn't much you can do about your situation, honey. The Bible teaches wives to submit to their husbands. If you submit to him and just keep on loving him, he'll eventually change into a godly husband. If he doesn't, well, that's too bad. I guess that's a burden God expects you to bear. Make God your husband. Oh, and keep praying.

This is the same wimpy, walk-all-over-me message that most Christian authorities give to the victims of adultery! It won't work with adulterers, and it won't work with a husband who is mistreating you in other areas.

Several of these wives said that they were told by well-meaning advisors to follow the thirty-day "Just Love Your Man" exercise. The idea here is to dedicate yourself for one month to ignoring your husband's sins and overwhelming him with loving behaviors. Give him affection and sex. Feed him like a king. Fetch his slippers. Rub his back. When he treats you like yesterday's garbage, just smile and carry on. Just be the best little wife in the whole world. At the end of the month, you'll have a brand-new husband. He'll respond to your love with his own love. He'll be so grateful to you for all you've done, he'll change completely.

I told these women, "That's the dumbest thing I've ever heard. Continuing to love him without expecting anything back is exactly what you've been doing for most of your marriage. It hasn't worked yet, so why would more of the same work now?"

These wives admitted the thirty-day love fest hadn't worked, and they had continued to feel totally unfulfilled and had become even more depressed and discouraged.

UNDERSTANDING HUSBAND NATURE

I explained to these wives that the "you must submit and unconditionally love" approach is a complete misunderstanding of the nature and mind-set of a sinning husband. (Furthermore, it fails to help good and loving husbands who, because of ignorance or background or erroneous teaching, are blundering in their treatment of their wives.) He is blinded by his sin (and Satan) and may not realize he's causing damage to himself, you, and the children. In fact, very often he believes he's a good guy and has a good marriage. He believes this because you, his wife, are still doing everything for him and have relinquished your rights to love and care and protection. As long as you keep meeting his needs and "submitting" to him and his sin, he thinks everything's fine.

If you seem okay with what's happening in the marriage, he's okay with it. He's pretty happy and will even convince himself that you're pretty happy. Many husbands can live quite contentedly in marriages with almost zero intimacy and emotional closeness. Wives and husbands who truly love each other "train" each other about what pleases them and what displeases them. Loving wives and husbands respond to this training and more and more fill each other's needs. This is not happening in these marriages, and the husbands I'm describing here don't know what they're missing. You do.

You can even tell your husband how unhappy you are, but he won't believe you if you continue to tolerate his sinful behavior and meet his needs. Your words mean nothing to him. He notices and perceives your behavior as acceptance—if not approval—of his treatment of you. You have surrendered your right to show your husband what your God-ordained, normal, deep needs are and your expectation of having them met.

Without realizing it you are enabling him to sin. You are encouraging him to sin. You are part of the problem. As long as you allow him to sin and help him stay comfortable in his sin, he may do a few nice things for you now and then. He'll toss you a few bones. Just enough to make you think he'll genuinely change. But he won't change! You make his life too easy, so he has no need to change.

GOD SAYS HE'S SINNING

"It's time to throw out the bad advice you've been given and take a look at what God says," I told each of these wives. God says your husband is involved in serious sin; he is disobeying a primary command of God—a command that is basic to God's creation, marriage and family. His behavior—being lazy, clearly disobeying such commands as those found in 1 Timothy 5:8 and 2 Thessalonians 3:10, failing to show love to you, neglecting you and the children, lusting, drinking to excess, sinning with the tongue, physically assaulting you (the opposite of touching you with great gentleness), controlling and dominating you—is sin in and of itself. Scripture clearly calls these behaviors sin.

His behavior is sin because it violates God's instructions—commands—to all husbands. He's certainly not loving you "just as Christ also loved the church and gave Himself up for her" (Eph. 5:25). He is not showing this sacrificial love—loving *as Christ loved the church* and *died* for her. He is not loving you as he loves his own body, as himself (Eph. 5:28–29, repeated in v. 33). He's not leading you in a loving, Christlike way as this passage—Ephesians 5:22–29—and Paul's words in Colossians 3:19 command him. He's not leading you as your head *in the same way* Christ is *his* head (Eph. 5:23). He's not, as Ephesians 5:28–29 commands him, meeting your needs in a very tender, caring manner.

In these passages God defines a husband's love for his wife. Your husband isn't even close to God's definition. He's much closer to the opposite.

In his first epistle, in giving basic instructions to husbands, Peter added a devastating message to husbands who treat their wives poorly: "You husbands likewise, live with your wives in an understanding way, as with a weaker vessel, since she is a woman; and grant her honor as a fellow heir of the grace of life, so that your prayers may not be hindered" (3:7).

God wants husbands to understand and do their part in meeting the spiritual, emotional, and physical needs of their wives. Husbands are to treat their wives with gentleness, honor, and respect, *treasuring* and *cherishing* them. Husbands who fail to do so in disobedience of God's commands will be spiritually cut off from God! Their line of communication to God will be disrupted!

This spiritual consequence is the worst thing that God could do to a husband. The withdrawal of fellowship with God is worse than physical, emotional, or career consequences. God takes very seriously a husband's care of his wife because it is the foundation of a good marriage and good parenting. God confronts the husband's sin in this area with a decisive and massive strike. So should you.

CONFRONT HIS SIN

Submitting to your husband's sin hurts him. It hurts you. It hurts the kids. It hurts your marriage. And it causes you to sin because you're not following the teaching of the Bible. What do you do with sin? You don't submit to it. You don't enable it. You fight it. You *confront* it. Read Chapter 12 of this book again. God certainly wants you to confront adultery. He also wants you to confront *all other serious sins* in your husband's life.

Your sinning husband will change only when he has to. When he's in pain and crisis. When he knows you will no longer enable or hide or be silent about his sin. When you follow the Bible's instructions to expose his sin and hit him with serious consequences. When he has lost you.

You have no idea the power and influence you can wield as a wife. Use them! God wants you to use them.

I know a husband is willing to finally address his sin when he comes into therapy and tells me: "Doc, I think I've lost her." At first, he'll work just to win you back. Along the way, he'll genuinely change. He'll own his problem and overcome it for himself and for God.

Just a brief message to a spouse who has been the abusive one in the marriage. If your behavior has caused your mate to no longer love you, then that's your fault, and your job is not to confront your partner's sin. You are the sinner, and now you must repent and work hard to win back your spouse. If you follow the steps I recommend for the sinning spouse in Chapter 16, you'll have the best chance to rekindle your partner's love.

How do you confront a sinning husband? You probably won't be too surprised when I tell you it's the same basic slam-his-hand-in-the-door approach I've described for dealing with an adulterous spouse. There are a few new wrinkles, however. Let me explain exactly what I want you to do.

SIXTEEN

A Battle Plan to
Change Your Marriage

*Stop Enabling and Make Your
Spouse's Sin the Issue*

Are you sick and tired of being mistreated by your husband? Are you weary of feeling depressed and devastated by his ongoing rejection of you? Are you through taking his abuse? Have you finally had it with his refusal to love you and be the kind of husband you want and need? If you answered yes to these questions, it's time to get to work. It's time to go to war.

There are reasons why you tolerate his disgraceful, damaging treatment of you. Your job is to find out what these reasons are and work on them. When you are healthy and assertive, you automatically change the rules of the dysfunctional relationship with your husband. This is the Preparation Phase of the war: working on yourself and getting ready for battle.

There are reasons why your husband doesn't love you and remains stuck in his sinful behavior pattern. Sin doesn't just happen. It has roots. It has sources. When you're strong enough, you can force him to face his sin and decide to continue it or stop it. This is the Offensive Phase of the war: confronting your husband with his sin and motivating him to do something about it.

Before we get into my Battle Plan, I want you to understand one thing. You are now operating independently of your husband's authority and leadership. His serious sin has disqualified him from his position of headship. As I hope I made clear in the previous chapter, you are not to submit to sin. You are not to encourage and support it in any way. You are to go to war with it and with the person who's committing it.

You will not ask your husband's permission to take the specific steps in my Battle Plan. Good thing, because it's likely he'll hate what you're doing and fight you tooth and nail. He'll be desperate to stop you because he wants to protect and nurture his sin. He wants to guard his flawed view of himself and his reputation. His angry, defensive reaction will just confirm that you're on the right track.

My Battle Plan will give you the best chance to bring real change and intimacy to your loveless marriage. I firmly believe it's what God wants you to do.

Step One: Get Close to God

This step almost goes without saying, but I'll say it anyway. You are going into spiritual warfare against Satan and what your husband is doing, so you must have the Lord by your side every inch of the way. Never forget that, when dealing with sin and the enemy of our souls, you are fighting not flesh and blood, but "spiritual forces of wickedness" (Eph. 6:12), and you will need to put on the "full armor of God" (Eph. 6:11, 13). You will need to be "strong in the *Lord*" (Eph. 6:10, emphasis added). Since you are on His side, the battle and the outcome are not yours; they are the Lord's, as David proclaimed before he killed the giant, Goliath (1 Sam. 17:47). The Lord will fight with you, for you, and through you *if* you are closely connected to Him.

Spend time each day alone with your heavenly Father, praying and reading His Word, and just being quiet and meditating over what you read. Attend church faithfully—not only services, but also Bible studies. When you are in an intimate relationship with God, Ephesians 6:10–11 will be a reality in your life: "Finally, be strong in the Lord, and in the strength of His might. Put on the full armor of God, that you may be able to stand firm against the schemes of the devil."

Step Two: Gather a Support Team

No one goes into a major battle alone. If you do, you won't have a chance. You'll be cut to ribbons in no time at all. Carefully select a small group—a platoon—of family members and friends who will go into battle with you. At least two of these fellow soldiers should live in your local area.

Gather your platoon members and tell them the entire truth about your husband's sinful behavior, your role in enabling it, the ways it has affected you, and just how bad your marriage is. Ask for regular prayer. In fact pray regularly with your small group of trusted supporters. In addition to spiritual support, ask for emotional and financial support. Ask these faithful warriors to push you to be strong and to press the attack against your husband's sin. Ask them to be there whenever you need them. Be sure to keep them apprised of how things are going in answer to their prayers.

Step Three: Work on Your Individual Problems

Find a highly skilled, experienced, licensed, and committed Christian therapist and begin a course of individual treatment. I understand that you may be very resistant to this idea. All I can tell you is that I think you'll dramatically increase the chances of getting the outcome you want if you do it anyway. Seeing a pastor or lay counselor won't be good enough. The stakes are too high, and the work too difficult and complex. No matter how spiritual and well-meaning a nonprofessional counselor may be, he or she does not have the training and skills necessary for your situation. You may certainly have helpers like these on your support team for prayer coverage, but do not look to them for specific guidance in therapy. Go to a specialist. It will cost, but it will be money well spent.

You want two things from your therapy. First, insight into why you have tolerated your husband's sin. What are the reasons you have been unable to stand up to your husband and demand change? Is it how you were raised? Is it a distant, uncaring, reject-ing father? Is it abuse you suffered as a child? Is it a transfer of unresolved pain and guilt from an abortion, premarital sex, or some other secret sin? Is it a lack of full recovery from a divorce? Is it poor self-esteem or a passive, compliant personality? Is it the incorrect teaching of your church on submission?

With God's guidance and a good Christian therapist, you can find out what the *it* is that is causing you to be an enabler and a victim of your spouse's sin. It may be one or more of these pos-sibilities I've listed. When you discover why you enable, you'll be able to do the work that will make you an emotionally healthy, assertive wife. A wife who will draw a line in the sand and say, "This far and no farther." A wife who will stop her part in the sin-ful marital pattern, force her husband to be all alone in his sin, and help him find his way to spiritual and emotional health.

The second thing you want from your therapy—your thera-pist—is a tough, take-no-prisoners, biblically sound approach. Don't waste your time and money with a therapist who recom-mends a weak, wimpy, "just love him and pray a lot" strategy. You want a therapist who will agree with my basic Battle Plan.

You want a therapist who will train you for war and guide you through it.

STEP FOUR: GET ANGRY

As I discussed thoroughly in Chapters 5 and 6, in order to be strong and courageous, you have to be angry. Even though you're not dealing with an adulterous spouse, he's still in serious sin, and you need to get angry. Now is not the time to forgive your husband. That comes later. In fact, expressing your anger is the first step on the road to forgiveness. If you don't get angry and do all you can to battle your husband's sin, you will never be able to forgive him. Unresolved resentments and regrets about your passive role as a victim will smolder inside for the rest of your life.

You're going into a battle for your marriage and family. You want to be pumped up. You want to be cold, hard, and determined. You want to be angry. An angry soldier is a whole lot more effective than a sad, depressed, insecure, "understanding" soldier. When you tap into your God-given anger for your husband's abusive and/or neglectful behavior, you'll be able to "take up the full armor of God, that you may be able to resist in the evil day, and having done everything, to stand firm" (Eph. 6:13).

Reread Chapters 5 and 6 and follow my instructions on how to get angry and stay angry. Just insert your husband's particular sin wherever I mention adultery in these chapters and follow the same basic steps to get your anger going.

STEP FIVE: GET PREPARED FINANCIALLY

When you confront your husband and stop playing your part in his sin, the situation could get ugly. It's very common for a sinning husband to retaliate by squeezing his wife financially. If he can swing it, you'd better expect him to cut off the money as a way of punishing you, shutting you up, and trying to get you back into the codependent role.

To make sure you'll have money for you and the children, follow the advice I gave in Chapter 11. Although yours is not an adulterous spouse, you have to take the same steps. Ask family, friends, and church leaders to be ready to help you with money. (Don't expect help from those who think you should quickly and easily accept the sinning husband back. And don't be discouraged by what they advise.) Also, arrange a place to stay if you and the kids need to leave the home temporarily, but do this only if your attorney advises it.

You're now ready to enter the Offensive Phase of the war with your husband and the spiritual war with the devil and the forces of evil. You're going to obey the Bible (see Chapter 12) and force your husband to directly face his sin. You're going to follow the same procedure—with a few changes that I described for dealing with an adulterous spouse. Before I tell you exactly what to do, here are two important exceptions to my standard procedure.

First, if you have any fear that your husband will have a verbally and/or physically violent reaction to your confrontation, don't do it alone (and, of course, be sure the children are nowhere near you). Have three supporters, at least two of whom are men (preferably large men), with you during the confrontation. Let one of the men do all the talking for you. If you don't fear an intense, scary reaction, but still don't feel up to facing this extremely difficult encounter alone, ask two or three others to be with you. At least one should be a man.

Second, if your husband has physically abused you or the children *in any way* or threatened to harm you or the kids, don't confront him in person. Make plans in secret—consulting with your attorney—for your financial support and a place to stay. Then follow a secret plan and leave your home with your children as soon as possible. Give him no warning. Just go. Don't tell him where you are going. Take the clothes you will all need for an extended stay.

Call the police and file a restraining order against your husband. File criminal charges of domestic violence/battery and do not retract them. You can send him a letter explaining in detail what he'll have to do to win you and the kids back. Staying with a man who has physically assaulted you is foolish and extremely dangerous. Don't do it. Get your children and get out quickly.

STEP SIX: CONFRONT YOUR HUSBAND

Tell your husband—in person, on the phone, or in a letter—that you have something very important to discuss with him. State clearly that the future of your marriage is at stake. Inform him you want to have this private meeting within twenty-four hours. Name the time and the place. It'll probably be in your home. Say nothing more. Just end the conversation or letter.

Do not tell him what it's about, no matter how much he badgers you. He knows what it's about. Make him wonder what you'll say. Make him sweat. Stay cool and pulled back until the meeting. If he's a bona fide crumb, he won't care at all. But if there's anything good left in him, he might just feel pressure and fear and guilt. That's what we want.

Ask your support team to pray hard before and during the meeting. At the appointed time and place, sit down with your husband and confront him with his sin. Have *everything* you are going to say written down—an account of what he has done that has harmed you or the children, your feelings, and what you require him to do to save the marriage. It's a lot easier to read than to remember everything you want to say. Plus, after the meeting, you'll hand him a copy of what you read. He will now know exactly the pain he has caused you and the children, how he has harmed the marriage, and what you expect him to do.

Ask him to be silent until you have finished reading your statement. If he keeps interrupting you, hand the letter to him and walk away. If he refuses to listen to you, just hand the letter to him and walk away. If he gets belligerent and hostile, hand the letter to him and walk away. You're not going to listen to even one more stupid rationalization, defensive comment, or sarcastic barb. After you've read the letter to him, if he doesn't immediately show signs of brokenness and agree to all your conditions, hand the letter to him and walk away.

Your statement/letter will open with a brief preamble in which you describe his sin and your decision not to tolerate it anymore. Then comes the meat of the letter: a list of nonnegotiable actions you expect him to fulfill.

I've included a sample letter of confrontation delivered by Shawna to her husband, Mike, the verbal abuser I described in the previous chapter. You may use the same format when you write your letter and confront your husband. Just plug in your husband's particular sin and specific behaviors.

Mike:

For the past ten years you have verbally abused me and our kids over and over. Your unpredictable temper and moods have caused me and them terrible damage. It's your words—your vicious, critical, sarcastic, mean words—that have cut us the most deeply. I don't know why you are so angry, and I don't care. I just want your verbal outbursts to stop—forever. I have allowed your sin of anger and verbal abuse to continue all these years. I've tolerated it. I've enabled it. That's my fault. I guess I was hoping and praying that somehow you'd change.

I'm through tolerating your anger and your verbal attacks. That's over with now. I have had it with your mouth. You can choose to continue your sin, but now there will be consequences. Serious consequences. I will not live with a man who rips and tears at his family.

The first consequence has already happened. You've lost me. You're not my hero or my knight in shining armor anymore. You're not my lover and sweetheart anymore. You've acted as though you hate me. If you want to win me back, you have a lot of work to do. If you choose to confess and repent of your sin, change, and try to win me back, here's what you have to do:

With your hand on the Bible, you will admit your sin to me and commit to do whatever it takes to change.

You will see _____, a Christian therapist, in regular sessions (weekly, at first) to work on your problem. We'll meet with the therapist together for the first three sessions or so.

You will confess your sin in a letter to me in which you will describe in detail the outbursts of temper you've had with me and the kids. You'll tell the specifics of as many outbursts as you can remember: the stressors and the events leading up to the outbursts, what happened during the outbursts, and the aftermath.

After you've read your letter to the therapist and me, I'll write a letter to you expressing all my resentments for your abusive, rotten treatment of me. After I've read my letter to the therapist and you, we will go through a period where I will vent my emotions to you and ask questions. You will listen, you will reflect, you will say you're sorry, and you will answer all my questions.

You will read Dr. Clarke's book cover to cover and do what he says to help me heal and to help you genuinely change. He explains all these steps of recovery in greater detail than I am doing in this letter.

You will see the therapist in individual sessions and do the personal work required to learn how to control your temper and stop your verbal abuse problem. You'll deal with your family of origin issues and past pain in your life. You'll study your addictive temper pattern and dismantle it.

You'll write letters to your parents and others who hurt you while you were growing up. You'll tell family and friends the truth and apologize for lying and blaming me.

You'll clean out all resentments you've harbored toward me and anyone else.

You'll do everything the therapist asks you to do. You'll sign a release so the therapist can update me on your progress.

You'll attend an anger management group for as long as your therapist and I believe it is necessary. [Note: there are Christ-centered recovery groups for anger, sexual addiction, substance abuse, and other problems in many locations.]

You'll meet regularly with a spiritual mentor. Here's his name and phone number: _____. He'll help you grow spiritually. You'll see him until he says you're ready to stop.

Also, you'll be accountable to one man for your temper for the rest of your life. You've got two weeks to find this man. He is subject to my approval. Both your spiritual mentor and your spiritual accountability guy will have your permission to tell me how you're doing.

For at least six months, you will attend a small discipleship group that meets at our church. You'll attend all the regularly scheduled services at our church. [Note: if your husband is not a Christian, he will still follow all these spiritual steps. You'll require him to study the Bible, meet with godly men, and seriously consider the claims of Jesus Christ. There will be no better opportunity for him to come to Christ than during this desperate crisis.]

If you do well in all these areas, I will agree to join you in marriage counseling with the therapist. We will both look at our parts in the *marriage* problems and work hard to build a healthy relationship. *You* will change first, and then we can work on the marriage.

Keep in mind, I won't argue about any of these points. You have to do them all. And the only person who will judge your progress and decide you've done enough is me.

Shawna

Wait for his reaction. If he immediately seems broken and contrite, hear him out. Stay cold and aloof, however. Tell him that words are cheap, and you've heard his promises before. This time, you want action.

If—as is likely—he does not respond well, hand him the letter and walk away.

STEP SEVEN: TAKE ACTION AGAINST HIS SIN

Don't tell your husband this, but give him one week to demonstrate brokenness and begin to comply with your requirements. As is the case when adultery is involved, his attitude and his behavior will reveal the condition of his heart. Whether he works hard to change, immediately after reading your letter of confrontation or not, you will take action to counteract his sinful behavior. In other words, you will provide consequences for his sin.

If your husband has been involved in a secret sin (sexual addiction, drugs, gambling), telling the children depends on your husband. If he's on board in the recovery process and doing well, you won't have to tell them about Dad's sinful behavior and what you're going to do about it.

However, if your husband resists and he refuses to work the program you've laid out, you must tell the children what he has done and the steps you're taking against his behavior. Make it clear to them that your goal is to help him, to try to make him stop his behavior. Reread Chapters 10 and 11 for the full explanation of why you tell your children the truth. Of course, if his sin has been obvious to the kids (temper, violence, verbal abuse and bad language, job trouble, workaholism, controlling behavior), you ought to go ahead and explain what you'll be doing to fight Dad's sin. In your explanation to the children, you must show that your hatred is not for him but for things he has done.

To make it clear what I mean by consequences, I'll tell you what the wives of the husbands of the previous chapter did:

Mr. Lazy

Carol took over the finances. All the accounts had only her name on them. Jim had no checkbook, no ATM card, and no debit or credit cards. Carol gave him a weekly allowance. He had to get a job—any job—and stay with it. His paychecks went into her checking account by direct deposit. If he lost a job because of laziness or poor work performance, he would leave the house for at least one month.

The Workaholic

Pam instructed Bob to tell her every day when he planned to get home within a twenty-five-minute estimate. He would not work at home unless it was a genuine emergency. He had regular, daily chores to do around the home. He dropped off the kids at school each morning, which gave him an excellent opportunity to talk with them. If he was later getting home than the previously agreed upon time, there would be no dinner made for him. If he was late to a school event or to church, he could not sit with her, and no one in the family would talk to him until they were back home.

The Sex Addict

Steve watched television only when Janet was with him. Janet had the password to the computer changed so only she knew it, and he could go online only when she was present in the home. He couldn't even go online for three months. If he was caught looking too closely at a woman, he slept on the couch that night. If he used any pornography of *any* kind— "mild" or hard core—and did not tell Janet immediately but she found out later, he would leave the home for at least one month. If, after he returned, Janet discovered he had looked at pornography again, he would leave the home for an indefinite period. And he would agree to enter long-term therapy.

The Alcoholic

Larry could not drink a drop of alcohol. Period. He took Antabuse, a medication that makes one violently ill if any alcohol is ingested. He ended his friendship with his drinking buddies. If he brought any alcohol home, Susan would pour it down the sink immediately. If he came home with alcohol on his breath, or he was caught drinking, he'd leave the house for at least one month. If he touched alcohol in that period of time, the month would be extended. His attendance at one meeting of a twelve-step program each week was compulsory.

Mr. Mouth

Shawna spoke up and immediately reprimanded Mike every time he mouthed off. And each time, she waited for him to admit it and apologize immediately. If he verbally abused the kids, she called him on it on the spot and demanded he apologize. In addition, for every slip of his tongue, he had to do a nasty household chore such as clean a toilet, clean the tub or shower stall, mop and wax the kitchen floor, or clean out the gutters.

The Violent Man

Sharon took the kids and left Bill. She pressed charges and filed a restraining order. She would not live with him again until he had proved real change over a six-month period.

The Controller

Denise demanded to see where all the money was. She got her name on all the financial accounts—checking, savings, retirement. She got a checkbook and an ATM card. She developed a list of chores that Frank would do around the home. If he complained about any job she had done, she wouldn't do that job for one week. *He* would do that job that week.

By the way, there was one other consequence every one of these wives imposed: no sex for at least the first month after the confrontation. Let me tell you, that can get a man's attention. If you keep giving him sex, you're enabling him, and he will think everything's fine. But it's not just about motivating him to change. It's about protecting a woman from serious emotional harm. When a woman continues to have intercourse with a man who's abusing her (and in my opinion, all of these husbands were abusing their wives), it damages her self-esteem, her integrity, and her emotional stability. To put it bluntly, it rips her guts out. God is not pleased with this kind of sex, and He doesn't want you to allow yourself to be used in this way. It violates one of the primary purposes of this blessed gift of God to husbands and wives.

STEP EIGHT: CONFRONT WITH WITNESSES

If after one week your husband is resisting your requirements, confront him again with two or three witnesses. Don't warn him ahead of time. Just invite your supporters to the home and do the intervention. Ask one of your team members, a man, to tell your husband he is sinning and needs to repent and do everything on the list you gave him.

STEP NINE: ASK THE CHURCH TO CONFRONT

If he does not immediately respond positively to step eight (confrontation), go to your church leaders and ask them to confront your husband and follow the Matthew 18 guidelines for church discipline. If they don't move quickly, or if your husband refuses to meet with them, go immediately to step ten.

STEP TEN: SHUN AND SEPARATE

If your husband chooses to reject all these biblical steps of confrontation, your responsibility to the Lord and the Bible is to follow the final command of Matthew 18. You are to shun the sinner and then separate from him. This gives him one final opportunity to come back to God and to you. It also provides protection for you and your children and prepares you for a life without your husband. Keep your children fully informed of what you are doing and why. You will follow the same shunning and separation plan I outlined in Chapters 10 and 11 for the wife of the adulterer. Your husband is in the same serious sin category as an adulterer, so you have to deal with him the same way.

I hope and pray you're tired of tolerating your husband's lack of love and his abusive treatment. You really don't have to put up with it anymore. My Battle Plan will lead you to a much better life. And maybe—just maybe—your husband will choose to stop sinning and become a much better man and spouse.

SEVENTEEN

YOU HAVE NOTHING TO LOSE AND EVERYTHING TO GAIN

With God's Help
Put Matthew 18 Love to Work

I know my approach is very difficult to carry out. When the man you love is involved in serious sin, it's incredibly hard to aggressively confront his behavior. My program is pretty close to the exact opposite of your natural impulses and the advice you'll get from most Christian sources. And yet it is the only plan I've ever seen produce successful results.

As I've worked to convince thousands of victimized spouses to use my *beyond* tough love approach, I've found that three final questions usually make up the last wall of their resistance. They are good questions, and they deserve to be answered.

Q: How can I follow your approach when I still love him?

A: I know you still love him. I don't want you to stop loving him. I want you to love him with an aggressive, confrontational love. The kind of love God exercises toward His children (Heb. 12:5–11) and the kind you would exercise with your child involved in gross sin, in the clutches of the devil, about to fall into the pit (Prov. 13:24;

23:13–14; Eph. 6:4). I want you to follow the Bible's instructions on how to love a person caught in serious sin. Refusing to tolerate his sin by confronting it is the most loving thing you will ever do for him. Often, a husband's very eternal soul and the souls of his children are saved in this process. Many a child has turned his back on God because of a sinning father. Even more daughters and sons have turned to God because of the influence of a godly father, including a father who sinned but acknowledged, confessed, repented of his sin, and was restored.

Is it *love* to sit back and allow him to destroy himself, your marriage, and your family? Your job is to try to tear your spouse from Satan's clutches and the utter destruction that will result if he keeps sinning. Maybe the Matthew 18 approach won't restore your husband, but it's your best hope, and God wants you to try it. All you can do is your part. The rest is up to your husband.

Picture your sinning husband in a car racing along a country road toward a cliff. It's a sheer drop of five hundred feet to the rocks below, but he doesn't realize the road ends in that cliff. He does, however, see you and the children standing in the road ahead of him. If you continue to love him in a wimpy, weak, do nothing, "only wait upon the Lord" way, it's like staying on the road with your kids in his path. He'll run over you and his family and then finally drive his car over the cliff.

If you get tough with your love and apply my program, you get yourself and the children off the road and to safety. You also warn him of the approaching cliff and do everything you can—taking very drastic, desperate action—to get him to stop. He may still choose to go over the cliff, but though it is a great loss, at least he destroys only himself. And you know you did everything you could to save him.

Speaking of your love for your husband, you'd better fight back with strong countermeasures while you still have some love for him left. If you wait and continue to accept his abuse with a forced little smile in the name of love or submission, your love for him will be gone eventually. As you let him chip away chunks of your love, resentment will grow and grow inside you. One day, you'll wake up and realize you don't love him anymore. You'll have no feelings for him at all. A terrible, numbing coldness will fill your heart. Under the coldness there will be the ashes of a love that was once vibrant and beautiful, and a huge hole filled with once happy memories that now bring only sadness instead. And all you'll be left with is a huge pool of smoldering resentments.

And then you won't care what he does. Even if he does all the right things, and does actually change, and his love for you seems to be restored, your response will be: "I couldn't care less." It's still possible for him to win you back, but it's very unlikely once you don't care anymore. Don't let this happen to you! If you love him in a weak, enabling way, you'll hit the wall and have absolutely no love left for him. Protect your love by pulling back from him and forcing him to face consequences for his sin. That way, *if* he does break and repent, you'll still be able to care and respond to his genuine changes.

Many husbands—clients and family and good friends— have told me that having their wives stand up to them when they acted badly made them become men their families are proud of. "Behind every good man there is a good woman" is solid truth, borne out in the lives of multitudes of men.

Q: What if he has always been a good and caring husband, is not having an affair, is not into any obvious sinful behavior pattern, but has recently pulled back from me and says he doesn't love me the way he used to?

A: He used to be a good and caring husband, but he's not one anymore. This is not the man who loved you deeply, pledged his lifelong care to you, and would have given his life for you. You must accept this terrible new truth and act accordingly. Your new, different husband is insulting you. He's harming you and the children. As I discussed in "God Says He's Sinning" (see Chapter 15), he is sinning in a serious, significant way. When he tells you he doesn't love you as he used to, he is directly violating God's command and His instructions to husbands about how to treat their precious soul mates.

And since love is—among other things—something you *do,* unexpressed love is not complete, biblical love by a long shot. With your tacit approval your husband has not been showing his love for you, *has not been doing the things that make love grow.* A plant that is deprived of sunshine, water, and nutrients shrivels and dies. When love is neglected, the sad results are predictable.

Disobeying God's commands to love and cherish his wife is only one of the sins your husband is committing. Believe me when I tell you that he is sinning in at least one other major area.

One distinct possibility is that he is on the verge of an affair or is in an adulterous relationship now. As bad as his admission that he does not love you as he once did, is the question of how long he has felt this way. The longer it has been, the more likely he has turned to someone else he could "love." Another possibility is that he is engaging in some secret sin such as viewing pornography (which would dissipate his sexual feelings for you), abusing drugs, or gambling. I've covered these two circumstances in detail. You know what to do.

The third possibility, and a very common one, is that your husband has never worked to develop a deep emotional and spiritual bond with you—especially in the vital area of communication. He has held in his emotions. He has not expressed his thoughts and feelings to you. He has been a poor communicator and has not done anything to improve his skills in this critical area. He hasn't shared with you the daily stresses of his job. He has chosen to stuff all the painful things that have happened to him in his life. He really hasn't grown much spiritually and has not revealed to you how he's doing in his relationship with God.

Many a good man spends years not being intimate on an emotional and spiritual level with his wife. He chooses this behavior, and according to the Bible, he is sinning. He won't let his wife or anyone else into his personal world. The result is, he is empty inside, and his needs for connection and passion go unmet.

He is like a time bomb waiting to go off. He doesn't know it, and you don't know it until one day when his emotional lone-ranger style catches up with him. He suddenly realizes he's miserable and terribly unfulfilled in his life. Of course he is! For years, he has completely shut out the one person designed by God to meet important needs: you, his wife.

He opens his mouth and tells you, "I don't love you anymore," or some variation of that horrible message. The fact is, he hasn't loved you the way he ought to have loved you (and the way the Bible teaches him to love you) all along. He doesn't know why he doesn't love you anymore. All he knows is that you "haven't met his needs," and he wants more out of life than your marriage is giving him. Literally thousands—millions—of husbands in this country say these words. They really don't understand why they don't love their wives anymore. And without ever learning why, they divorce at least one wife. This dummy fails to realize that he has never given you a chance to meet his needs!

In the blink of an eye, he goes from a good husband to a bad husband. From someone who cared about you, and at least treated you decently, to someone who is totally focused on himself and how to fill his bone-dry need tank. He won't just "snap out of it," either. You will have to shake him out of it. Or he will join the statistics listing the husbands who, sometimes out of ignorance, but still deliberately, ruin a marriage.

If you don't act to get his attention, he'll act in some sinful way to get his needs met. He'll find someone or something outside the marriage to satisfy his suddenly overwhelming desire for intimacy.

You'd better pull back and make him and his sin the issue, so that he will be forced to learn why he never found his needs met with you, and discover that he can. You'd better make him believe he has lost you. You'd better tell him he has set himself up for his current, sinful, unhappy, unfulfilled state. You'd better tell him if he wants you back to discover and cultivate what he never worked to find, he will have to get to work: on himself, on his relationship with the Lord, and on the marriage.

Q: What if he does not respond to Matthew 18 love?

A: What if he doesn't? You've lost nothing because you have nothing right now. Stop pretending to grasp at straws. All the straws are gone. He's gone. It's over. He said those climactic words: "I don't love you anymore." My program gives you the best opportunity to shock your husband back to God and you—to give him his, and your, only chance for him to learn what he has never learned in your marriage, and to love you again. If it doesn't work, and he continues to choose to follow Satan's plan for his life, no godly woman would want him in her life. And at least you've obeyed God and taken a stand.

If he chooses not to change, you'll forgive him and keep on forgiving him. That's what the Bible teaches you to do (Matt. 18:21–22; Col. 3:13). God doesn't want bitterness to destroy you. But you won't reconcile. You'll keep your heart, mind, and body away from him until he repents. You won't file for divorce, but you'll continue to shun and separate.

Remember those couples with the sinning husbands I described in the last few chapters? Four of the couples survived and built brand-new, healthy marriages. Two of the couples divorced, and one is currently separated. But I can tell you that the women and the children in the divorced and separated cases are all doing well. They're emotionally strong and walking with the Lord. They're sad, and they're grieving the loss of a dad and husband, but they're going to make it. They're going to rebuild their lives and move on to a new horizon that God has given them.

THE FINAL CHARGE

It's time for action. It's time for confrontation. It's time for biblical, Matthew 18 love. You have nothing to lose. You have everything to gain:

- the knowledge that you did all you could to create change
- the only real possibility of your husband's turning around
- a new life for you and your children
- a closer walk with God
- God's blessing on you

God willing, one day soon you'll hear these words from your spouse: "I love the Lord, I love you, and I'll do whatever it takes to win you back. I *do* love you." The one best chance you have to hear these words is to obey God and follow His strategy to confront and break your husband.

You can't do it alone. It's too much to ask. I know that. But you won't be alone. Claim Joshua 1:9 as your verse: "Be strong and courageous. Do not be terrified; do not be discouraged, for the LORD your God will be with you wherever you go" (NIV).

God will be with you every step of the way. God will help you do what you must do.

ABOUT THE AUTHOR

First and foremost, Dr. Clarke is a Christian. His personal relationship with Jesus Christ is the most important part of his life. His spirituality is the driving force behind everything that he does. He is a member of Christ Community Church, an independent Bible-teaching church in Tampa, Florida. Dr. Clarke has been married to his wife, Sandy, since 1982. They have four beautiful children: Emily (16), Leeann (14), Nancy (11), and William (7).

Dr. Clarke holds a B.A. in Psychology from Point Loma College in San Diego, California. He also holds an M.A. in Biblical Studies from Dallas Theological Seminary in Dallas, Texas. His Ph.D. is in Clinical Psychology from Western Conservative Baptist Seminary in Portland, Oregon.

Beginning in 1982, at a Minirth-Meier Inpatient Clinic in Garland, Texas, Dr. Clarke has trained in a number of inpatient hospitals and outpatient counseling centers. He is a licensed psychologist in the state of Florida. Since 1986, he has had a full-time private practice in Tampa seeing individuals, couples, and families in therapy. In addition Dr. Clarke has been an adjunct teacher at the Tampa extensions of Dallas Theological Seminary and Southeastern Baptist Theological Seminary.

Dr. Clarke is a popular speaker. His practical and entertaining seminars on marriage and parenting present God's truth about relationships.

OTHER BOOKS BY DAVID CLARKE

Men Are Clams, Women Are Crowbars

Winning the Parenting War

A Marriage After God's Own Heart

To schedule a seminar or order Dr. Clarke's books, audiotapes, and videotapes, please contact:

David Clarke Seminars
www.davidclarkeseminars.com
1-888-516-8844
or
Marriage & Family Enrichment Center
6505 North Himes Avenue
Tampa, Florida 33614

Printed in the United States
125644LV00001B/21/P